OPEN WATER SWIMMING: LESSONS FROM ALCATRAZ

JOE OAKES
&
GARY EMICH

PIANO! PIANO! PRESS

Requests for permission to make copies of any part of the work should be emailed to alcatrazjoe@hotmail.com or mailed to:
PIANO! PIANO! PRESS
3075 NW Montara Loop
Portland, OR 97229-8084.

Library of Congress Cataloguing-in-Publication Data
LCCN: 2010917808
Oakes, Joe
Emich, Gary
Open Water Swimming: Lessons from Alcatraz / Joe Oakes and Gary Emich – 1st edition
p. 135
ISBN: 978-0-615-42073-8

Text set in Adobe Garamond Pro
Cover and book design by John Morris-Reihl, www.artntech.com
Manufactured by Lightning Source, LLC

Text set in Adobe Garamond Pro
Cover and book design by John Morris-Reihl, www.artntech.com
Cover photo - Peg Gerard
Manufactured by Lightning Source, LLC

TABLE OF CONTENTS

DEDICATION

*If we have been able to accomplish anything in this world, it
is because of the constant and unselfish support of the two
women who have put up with us for so many years,
Pegie Gerard (Gary's wife) and Sylvia Nelson Oakes (Joe's wife.)
There are not enough words or ways to say thank you.*

FORWARD

TO OUR READERS: CAVEAT EMPTOR

Gary likes to say that there are only two kinds of open-water swimmers: Those who have met and overcome the challenges posed by swimming from Alcatraz and those who are still standing on the shore. This book is meant for both of them.

If you have this book in front of you, you have either made a serious error or you are interested in making an attempt to swim from Alcatraz Island to San Francisco. Assuming that the latter is correct, we want you to understand why we have gone to the trouble of writing the book. It is certainly not for the money.

First, we want to encourage anyone with sufficient desire and ability to enjoy the wonderful feeling of success that comes from completion of this great, difficult and classic swimming challenge. Alcatraz swims have been our obsession for many years. It is our hope that you will find in these pages both the information and the inspiration to turn your desire into reality. Read on and devour what we have prepared for you.

Second, over the past 30 years we have seen too many unqualified swimmers trying unsuccessfully to swim from Alcatraz. In that time our Alcatraz Safety Crew has had to rescue well over 1,000 swimmers, many of whom never should have been out there foolishly endangering themselves and those around them. If you suspect that you fall into that category, please do not attempt an Alcatraz swim until you fully understand the seriousness of the undertaking and have proven to yourself that this long, cold, rough water swimming challenge is within your capabilities. Bravado has its place, but not at Alcatraz.

Maybe that sounds too cold. Try to visualize how John Wayne might say it, "*Okay, Pilgrim. When you've done all the hard work and got yer stuff together, we'll be ready for ya.*" Or maybe Humphrey Bogart, quietly, a cigarette dangling from his lip, "*Think it over, Kid. This ain't no picnic.*"

Here's the bottom line: *Swimming from Alcatraz* is never an easy undertaking. Approach it with caution. When you have accomplished your goal, you will have done something worth a great effort.

JO

ABOUT THE AUTHORS

WHO THE HECK ARE THESE GUYS, ANYWAY?

That is a fair question. If I were picking up a book to learn about taking on a challenge I would want to know about the people who are professing to tell me what to do.

Gary Emich has completed more "clean" swims (sans wetsuit or fins) from Alcatraz than any living person. He currently has made over 750 crossings and has set his goal to being the first to reach 1,000. He is a certified Level 1 USA Triathlon coach specializing in open water and a Level 2 American Swimming Coaches Association coach. He personally has trained many aspirants to do the difficult swim from Alcatraz. If you want to learn more about Gary and what he does, visit *lanelines-toshorelines.com*.

Joe Oakes conceived the idea of putting on triathlons in San Francisco Bay after completing his first Ironman Triathlon in Hawaii in 1980. In the past 30 years Joe has directed over 30,000 swimmers in their quest to cross from Alcatraz to San Francisco. He was the first person to swim from Russia to Alaska and the only person to have completed both a full marathon and a long swim on every continent. Joe got his first Red Cross Water Safety Instructor's license in 1965. Before becoming a race director, Joe had a career as an engineer and a small business owner. For more information on Joe, go to *Josephoakes.com*. While you are on his website, buy his book, *With a Single Step*. 100% of the proceeds go to a group of AIDS orphans in Namibia.

PART ONE:

That Miserable Little Island.

Some Alcatraz History
Joe Oakes

"The sole purpose of Alcatraz was to degrade, humiliate and break the inmates physically, mentally and spiritually."

Jim Quillen – former inmate at Alcatraz
"Alcatraz From the Inside, The Hard Years"

Millennia ago the rocky island that we today call Alcatraz rose up from the surrounding San Francisco Bay, a minor result of the same plate tectonics that produced the Sierra Nevada. The island, extending southeast to northwest, is roughly a quarter mile long by 200 meters wide. Before the arrival of the white man Alcatraz Island was a place that local native people, the Miwoks and the Costanoans, relied on for their sustenance, gathering eggs, catching fish and snaring birds. Centuries before the American Declaration of Independence, Spanish *conquistadores* had already incorporated the region into *Nueva Espana*. San Francisco, then known as *Yerba Buena*, was a small Spanish outpost. The little island that we call Alcatraz was called Isla de los *Alcatraces* for the birds nesting there.

Even before the Gold Rush of 1849, *norteamericanos* were crossing the continent and settling in Mexican California, part of the American policy of 'manifest destiny.' In 1847 Alcatraz Island was purchased by Americans. With the onset of the Gold Rush San Francisco was deluged with non-Spanish speaking people, and eventually the Spanish population faded into a minority, from which status it has recently been recovering. With its diversity, there is no longer a majority population in California.

On August 27, 1861 Alcatraz Island was given to the US Army for use as a penitentiary, serving the needs of the Army in the Pacific area. It was a very unpleasant place. Military prisoners were attached to 24-pound iron balls by long steel chains. Flogging was common, as was branding, *D* for deserters, *T* for thieves. Just prior to World War I the US Army built a new military prison on Alcatraz, the Pacific Branch of the U.S. Disciplinary Barracks. Prisoners were euphemistically called *disciples*.

In the mid 1920s 15-year-old Walter Stack, a hungry, orphaned street kid from Detroit, joined the Army to get a regular meal ticket. He signed up for four years. The Army sent him to a post in the Philippines to serve his time. An impulsive, undisciplined kid, Walter decided that he did not like Army life and he simply walked away, wandering in the Philippines. When the Army caught up with him, Walter was convicted of desertion and sent to Alcatraz to serve a two year term, followed by discharge from the Army. He served his time and stayed in San Francisco until his death in 1990. I knew Walter in the 1970s and 1980s. He was a fine athlete, a natural leader and a tough old bird. Walter was one of the early swimmers from Alcatraz. Think about this: Walter completed his time on Alcatraz while Al Capone and his like were still petty criminals in Chicago, and Walter was still running marathons and swimming in San Francisco Bay long after the bad guys were pushing up daisies.

The Army turned Alcatraz over to the U.S. Justice Department in August of 1934. The Army's budget had been slashed during the Great Depression. The Justice Department was getting bad press because prisoners kept escaping from federal prisons. It was thought that the island fortress of Alcatraz would solve their dual problems of keeping prisoners in prison and the bad press that resulted from so many escapes. So in the 1930s the real bad guys started to take up residence as guests behind the 'impenetrable' walls of Alcatraz.

It did not quite work out that way. Prisoners did, in fact, escape, as we shall see later. It was very expensive provisioning and staffing a prison on a barren island. Eventually the government, under Attorney General Robert F. Kennedy, accepted reality and shut down Alcatraz Prison in 1963, not even 30 years after taking it over from the Army.

A few years later a man named Richard Oakes (no relation to me) led a group of similar minded Native-American activists in an occupation of Alcatraz. It was not a successful venture for them, and they gave up their quest after nineteen months of difficulties, including the accidental death of Oakes' young daughter. It did, however, succeed in focusing attention on the plight of Native Americans.

Alcatraz then sat abandoned and deteriorating in the Bay for several years until another Federal agency, the Golden Gate National Recreation Area (GGNRA) was created within the National Parks Service. The GGNRA's holdings include Alcatraz Island which has been developed into a tourist attraction. Today a private ferry service has a contract with the GGNRA to carry boatloads of tourists to Alcatraz every day, and tickets must be purchased in advance. The award-winning Alcatraz Cellhouse Audio Tour is narrated by the prisoners and correctional officers who actually lived there during the infamous Federal Penitentiary era and provides a picture of what life was like in the miserable cellblocks, as well as other strange tales of its long-ago residents.

There is a big sign on the south end of Alcatraz Island warning that anyone coming within 300 yards, three football fields, of the island would be in violation of the law and might be shot at or arrested. Few wanted to test the resolve of the prison's notorious guards. As a result, attempts to swim from Alcatraz were few. On October 18 1933, 17-year old Anastasia Scott became the first to swim from Alcatraz, completing her crossing in 43 minutes. It is believed that the first organized club swim was in 1963. My first swim from Alcatraz was in the 1970s. The first triathlon starting at Alcatraz took place in 1981, put on by Peter Butler, Sally Bailey and me. It was done as a fund raiser for the Dolphin Club. (That identical club event has been contested for 30 years as of this writing.) The next year we also put on a swim-run biathlon. Both events started out with a tiny handful of rugged individuals. Today these events have seen growth to the point where the demand for an entry far outstrips the available spots.

WHY WAS ESCAPE FROM ALCATRAZ SO DIFFICULT?

Escape from Alcatraz prison was, in fact, extremely difficult, the result of several factors, some unquestionably real, others existing primarily in the minds of the prisoners.

First, there were the very real factors that, when combined, presented formidable obstacles to any prisoner who had in mind to leave the island. Alcatraz was a heavily fortified prison with extraordinary guards. It was designed for a special class of prisoners. At Alcatraz 'maximum security' was practiced far more than at any other federal facility. When prisoners were not working, eating or at their very limited exercise periods, they were confined to their cells. The cell doors were made of heavy bars of hardened steel alloy, almost impossible to file or saw through. Beyond the cell doors, they would need to get through three additional security doors before exiting into the enclosed yard area.

If they made it out of the cell block and the building, there remained very high walls, which were topped by six guard towers and rows of barbed wire. At that point there would be a steep 40 foot drop down a ragged cliff to the water's edge. Guards in motorboats patrolled the water surrounding the island. The guards on the island were specially chosen for toughness. They were said to be both frightening and frightened by their charges.

If they made it to the water's edge they would then have to face crossing a mile and a half of frigid San Francisco Bay to the nearest point of land. The water was cold, deep and turbulent, with no shortage of sharks lurking not far from the island. In the minds of the prisoners, a swim across those waters would have a very small chance of success.

Prison scenes in modern movies show healthy prisoners pumping iron in the yard, jogging around, keeping themselves very fit. That is not how it was on Alcatraz. Exercise opportunities were minimal, let alone the chance to take a swim. They were not health nuts, they were habitual criminals. Without booze and women, their main vice was cigarettes. 'Exercise' and 'fitness' were not part of their way of thinking. The prison diet, as you might expect, was far from a healthy one.

But assuming that one of them made it into the cold, turbulent water, he would then face a gauntlet of traffic: fishermen headed in or out of the Gate; oil tankers, freighters, cruisers, barges and military vessels in the international shipping lanes both south and north of Alcatraz. A swimmer in the water is almost invisible to the pilot of a large vessel, and a six foot diameter propeller wouldn't even make a bump as it turned you into fish food.

(I can tell you from personal experience that when you are swimming in San Francisco Bay and a large ship is bearing down on you, it looks and feels like you are about to be run over by an out-of-control aquatic Empire State Building. The ship's pilot, hundreds of feet down the deck in the pilot house, ten stories above you, probably can't even see your nine-inch diameter, orange-capped head in the water. Even if he did see you it is impossible to stop or turn a large ship in a short distance. There is no way you can swim fast enough to get out if the way of that terrifying behemoth. I was fortunate that my pilot boat was close at hand and whisked me out of harm's way, not a moment too soon. The moral is obvious: never swim alone and always swim with a competent pilot.)

Invisible Specks to the Tanker Pilot
(Gary & Down Syndrome Athelete Karen Gaffney)

It was part of the job of the institution's guards and administrators to bring the prisoners to the belief that it would be impossible to escape. This was, after all, *Alcatraz*. Picture yourself contemplating an escape: You would have to get free of the bars, the security doors, the walls, the barbed wire, the sadistic guards in the gun towers, the patrol boats, and only then would you be in a position to swim through the perilous waters of San Francisco Bay, sharks, boats, currents and all.

In 1982 I met a man named John Quillen while visiting the former prison. John, in his 50's at the time, had served a sentence on Alcatraz as a very young man, hardly out of his teens. After 'graduation' from Alcatraz he built a life for himself, working and raising a family in the San Francisco area. John had written a book about his time behind bars. His depiction of the guards was one of cruel men working under stringent rules. One of the standing rules was to shoot to kill any inmate attempting to escape. He tells the story of one man, insane, trying to climb up an impossibly vertical wall in full view of several guards. The guards watched, laughing at him before taking their time to execute the poor lunatic with several well placed bullets. Killing him would be much easier than trying to subdue him, and it would serve as a good example for the other prisoners.

These prisoners, however, were desperate men, and they had little to lose. Life was miserable in cold cells that measured four feet by eight feet, furnished only with a cot, a seatless toilet, a sink, a small table, a chair and a light bulb hanging from the ceiling. The official 'Code of Silence' allowed conversation between prisoners only three minutes per day, one hour on weekends. Suicide was common among inmates. Some faked escape in order to be put out of their misery by the too-willing guards. Others slit their wrists or throats with crude knives made from sharpened spoons. There was good reason for them to call their home The Tomb of the Living Dead. It was inevitable that some of these desperate men would do anything, take any chance to free themselves from the misery of being incarcerated at Alcatraz.

WHAT WOULD IT BE LIKE TO ATTEMPT A SWIM FROM ALCATRAZ?

'Fortress Alcatraz' was the pride of the federal prison system. It was a showplace, the message being that the Feds had at last gotten their thumbs on organized crime.

Because of its remoteness, everything that was needed on the island had to be brought in by boat from the mainland. There were many applicants for the job of Alcatraz prison guard and only the very best were selected from the many for this prized position during the Great Depression. These guards were given the extraordinary power to put to death anyone attempting an escape. An inmate with escape in mind would have to be very clever, physically tough, resilient and extremely patient. The one thing they had on their side was time for detailed planning, plenty of time.

Is the water around Alcatraz really that bad? Alcatraz Island sits in the middle of San Francisco Bay forming an obstruction to the ever-moving currents. Twice a day the Pacific Ocean comes flooding into San Francisco Bay through the Golden Gate, just to the west of the island, as the gravitational action of the sun and moon combine to produce tidal pressures. After a few hours the whole process reverses and the water turns around and ebbs right back out the Gate into the Pacific. In-out-in-out, all day long, the currents are relentless except for the very brief times when they turn around, the so-called 'slack.' The velocity of the flooding and ebbing currents can be much greater than the swimming speed of Olympic caliber athletes, often reaching six or more knots. When the flowing water comes crashing up against the obstacle of Alcatraz in their path, it boils up and produces a complex swirl of water that is, to say the least, uninviting to a swimmer. Only at the brief slack tides does it quiet down enough to put fear aside for a few minutes.

A prisoner might become a student of the tides and currents. Careful observation over the months and years would educate him enough to draw the conclusion that entering the water during the flood tides would carry him eastward towards Oakland, while the ebb would take him to the west, towards the Gate. He might also note that the currents vary over the course of a lunar month, the greatest currents being at the full and new moons and the weakest at the half moon. It would not be far-fetched to reach the conclusion that the best time to take his leave would be on a slack tide near the time of a half moon. Of course he would have to get to the water first, no easy feat. But some of these guys were ingenious.

After reaching the water there would be the temperature to deal with. The water in San Francisco Bay rarely rises above 60 F and just as rarely falls below 49 F. It is *always* cold, but just exactly what does that mean to a human body? It is a common belief that a person falling into the Bay would have less than ten minutes to live. That is a lot of baloney. Swimmers from the great South End Rowing Club and the Dolphin Club routinely swim in that water daily, year round, never wearing anything more than an embarrassingly skimpy swim suit (not even that on their birthdays). On New Year's Day they swim from Alcatraz in water hovering around 50 degrees, some of them in the water for well over an hour.

The obvious question to ask is whether these swimmers were born with the ability to withstand cold water or whether they are normal human beings who have trained themselves to withstand the cold. The human body can withstand much more than we think it can. Several years ago a brave young Californian, Lynne Cox, challenged the waters of the Bering Strait, and in so doing she became the first person to swim from Alaska to Russia (Little Diomede to Big Diomede), not far from the Arctic Circle. The water temperature was in the high 30's and she was in that water for over two hours, wearing only a swim suit, a thin cap and goggles. In 1994, I became the first person to swim between the same two islands in the opposite direction (I, however, wore a wetsuit.) Michelle Macy, a good friend of mine, is planning to make the eastward swim in the Diomedes next year without a wetsuit if she can get permission from the Russians. Several Chileans have swum across the Strait of Magellan without wetsuits in water that is usually in the forties in the summer. There is a group of cold water swimmers in Portland, Oregon who go out every weekend, some swimming for several hours in water in the fifties. So, yes, it is possible for humans to survive in very cold water for a long time. It is made possible by training, by a bit of body mass, and by that wonder of modern technology, the wetsuit.

One of the challenges that members of the South End Club like to undertake is a *Round Trip Alcatraz (RTA)*. It is not just a swim to the island and back: the swimmer also has to circumnavigate the island, working around the rugged and irregular island in currents that are trying very hard to prevent it. Timing must be perfect, the tides just right and luck on your side. Wetsuits are not allowed. After a swim of over a mile getting to the island, there will be treacherous rocky out-croppings, fierce currents, whirlpools and back-eddies to negotiate on the back side of the island before turning around and swimming back to Aquatic Park and that wonderful life-restoring sauna. I piloted such a swim for the talented Canadian couple, Debbie and Shane Collins a while back. Old timer Frank Drum said it succinctly, paraphrasing the Bible: "Many are cold but few are frozen."

Gary will go into more detail about hypothermia, but let me say that I have seen many swimmers start shaking violently after reach-ing the beach. I recall professional triathlete Dean Harper finishing an Alcatraz swim as the first part of a 1982 triathlon. He mounted his bicycle and fell over, not once but three times. His reaction time was way off because of the cold water. Hypothermia is insidious. One of the symptoms is the inability to think straight, so when you are becoming hypothermic you just might not be aware of it. Your speech may become slurred, your reactions slow, and your senses working in a lower mode. You are out of sync with the real world, operating on a different frequency. Worse yet, you may come out of the water feeling fine, but after that cold blood that has accumulated just inside your skin starts to circulate back to your core, you can be in big trouble. What you have to do is get warm fast. Ditch the cold wetsuit and swim suit and get into a sauna. If there is no sauna, have someone turn your car heater to as hot as you can run it, which should take a few precious minutes. On occasion I have gone for a quick run to get my muscles generating heat. The point is that you should not sit around waiting for your body to return to normal: help it to warm up.

Summarizing, a person attempting to swim from Alcatraz could encounter very rough, choppy water. The water will be moving, but not necessarily in the direction that you want to go. It will be very cold, normally below 60 F. You will be in the water for at least a half hour, probably more like an hour depending on conditions and your fitness level. Your timing will have to be spot-on, and you had better know what the currents are doing at that exact time. If you succeed you will not be the first, and if you fail, you will be in good company.

Then there is the question of sharks. I am going to leave it to Gary to say more on the sharks of San Francisco Bay, but I will make one personal comment about them. There are plenty of sharks in San Francisco Bay. I have personally seen fishermen haul them in, thrashing and wildly protesting the indignity. The presence of sharks, even lesser species than the feared great whites, gives me a feeling of unease when I am sharing the water with them. So I simply choose not to think about them.

COULD A PRISONER HAVE MADE IT?

In 1991 I was asked that question by an interviewer from British Television BBC. More specifically, she wanted to know about Frank Lee Morris and the Anglin brothers, John and Clarence. Here is what I told her.

Prisoners on Alcatraz were not in especially good physical condition. They would certainly not be acclimated to cold water. The federal government was so sure that it was not possible that they made a major investment in Alcatraz, both financially and in the public perception. But despite their elaborate planning and hyperbole at least one prisoner is positively known to have fled from Alcatraz. Inmate

John Paul Scott actually did escape and swim from Alcatraz to the south anchorage of the Golden Gate Bridge at Fort Point on December 12, 1962. Was his escape attempt successful? Only partially, even though the prison guards didn't know that he was gone. But after he made landfall, he was hypothermic and barely able to climb up the rocky shore and could go no further. A boy saw the poor wretch, not knowing that he was an escaped prisoner, and summoned help in the form of the local gendarmerie, who kindly escorted him back to his home on The Rock. If John Paul Scott could make it in the middle of the winter, why couldn't others?

And then there is the interesting case of four prisoners who escaped from Alcatraz while it was still a US Army prison. They made good their escape on Thanksgiving Day, November 28, 1918, during the First World War. Using a makeshift wood raft, Andy Armen, Paul White, Fritz Isell and Herbert Koenig disappeared during a Thanksgiving Day celebration. The government tried to convince the populace that they had drowned, but two months later Koenig was located while partying in San Francisco. He told the authorities that all four had indeed made it to shore. The others were never apprehended.

The book, *Escape From Alcatraz*, in describing the escape of Frank Morris and the Anglin brothers blithely echoes the official sentiments of the prison officials, strongly stating that all three had undoubtedly drowned in San Francisco Bay. I disagree with them, and here is why: When a person drowns, after a few days the body comes to the surface because gas buildup makes it very buoyant. It is improbable that not one of the three bodies would rise, but none did. I therefore assume that they went somewhere other than to the bottom of San Francisco Bay.

I imagine that if one of them is still alive so many years later, he might still be chuckling over a cold drink someplace, relishing his grand deception and savoring the last days of a long run of blessed freedom. If I were in that situation I might just send a postcard from Rio or someplace safe, saying hi to the men who replaced J. Edgar Hoover and the G-Men. It would not surprise me if the escapee had actually done that, maybe several times, but the government would never tell us about it, would they?

HOW GOOD A SWIMMER DO YOU HAVE TO BE TO MAKE IT FROM ALCATRAZ?

Despite the dire warnings of the federal government when Alcatraz housed prisoners, it is not a very difficult swim for a reasonably accomplished swimmer. It certainly does not require an Olympic caliber athlete. In fact, over 5,000 swimmers make the swim every year. (That's a huge number compared to the year 1981 when I had to practically beg 13 swimmers to give it a try.) The fastest swimmers complete the trip in under a half hour. Slow swimmers may not reach land for over an hour. If you can swim a mile in cold, open water in 40 minutes, this swim should be within your grasp. Our success rate over the years has been in the range of 90%.

Caveat emptor: Guiding swimmers from Alcatraz has become a lucrative business for a few avaricious people, some of whom border on incompetence. For some there is a conflict between providing (costly) protection and maximizing profits. Make sure that your guide and the event production company have solid experience by checking out their reputations.

The reasons for the failure of some swimmers are varied, but usually are related to poor conditioning; insufficient preparation for cold water; unexpected conditions in the water; swimming in the wrong direction; or just plain fatigue. Repeating: over three decades we have had over a 90% success rate.

WHY DO YOU WANT TO SWIM FROM ALCATRAZ?

Here are a few things to think about. First, do you want to *swim* from Alcatraz or do you want to satisfy your curiosity? There are easier ways to visit (and leave) Alcatraz. Many hire a power boat, and there is no shortage of boat-for-hire outfits on Fisherman's Wharf who will take you out for a quick sniff. I love to take a kayak from the South End Club and circumnavigate the island, a three mile round trip. You can also go out on the ferry trips that leave daily. But you really want to swim, don't you?

The next thing to think about is whether you want your swim to be part of a race or should it be a solo affair. There are several advantages to being part of a large swim (look at the appendix for a few suggested events). It will probably cost you a lot less than hiring your own boat and doing a solo. You can also rely on a good race promoter to select the correct timing of the tides and currents, not a simple matter. And if you want company, or if you want competition in your quest, you might find several hundred like-minded individuals out there with you. (The standing joke is that your odds against a shark attack are much better when the beast has 1,000 bodies to choose from.) The organizers will not only give you a race but will also probably give you a neat tee shirt and something to fill your tummy when you reach the finish line. *Be forewarned: the good events fill up fast, so file your entry early.*

If cost is no object or the timing of the races does not fit your schedule, you might consider a solo crossing. You will find information on that in the appendix as well.

Okay, you know where you are swimming *from* (Alcatraz), but where will you be swimming *to*? From that little island you can swim to any point of the compass. What will determine the direction you select will be the tides and currents, which are many times stronger and faster than you are. Swimming in San Francisco Bay involves a partnership between your puny body and that gigantic bay, and the Bay makes the rules. With an ebbing current you will of necessity be swept to the west because that is where the huge mass of water is going. A flooding current will want to take you east. The key is to know what the water is doing and play along with Mother Nature. If you are determined to go in a specific direction, you will have to wait for the right tides and currents to help you get there.

How will you know when that will happen? Read the bible! In this case the bible is not the Good Book but the **tide tables** (see the Glossary) that have been empirically developed over the years by the National Oceanic and Atmospheric Administration (NOAA) in Washington, D.C. Reading and understanding the tide tables can be mastered, but it is a lot more complex than it appears at first glance. There are a few basic variables such as date, time, tide condition (the rise and fall of the water's surface), and currents (the horizontal movement of the water.) There are also some subtleties that are less easy to master, things like large variances that occur in different places in the Bay, even back-eddies that can actually move in the opposite direction to the main current. What I want to stress is that you had better have a thorough understanding of the tide tables or work with someone who knows what they are doing.

The standard South End and Dolphin Club destination for swims from Alcatraz has been for many years the cove at Aquatic Park on the north end of Van Ness, just to the west of Fisherman's Wharf. They finish there because both the South End Club and the Dolphin Club have their homes right on that cove. It is also the shortest physical distance from Alcatraz, being directly south of the island. However, swimming into Aquatic Park from Alcatraz is a tricky proposition. The best time to do it is in the middle of the lunar month around time of the neap tides, because that is when the currents are weakest. You will probably start about a half hour before the slack current at Alcatraz (*not* the slack at the Gate). Early mornings are best because there is usually less wind and less traffic. But *timing is critical and so is the route you choose to swim.* To enter Aquatic Park you must pass through a narrow opening at the end of the Municipal Pier. Miss it and you will be fighting currents and there is a strong possibility that you will not be able to make it into the cove. Because you are essentially crossing a big, moving river, the direction in which you swim to reach that narrow opening will depend on your swim speed: slower swimmers will have to take a more conservative route than the faster swimmers, the result being that they will of necessity be in the water longer. If you are unsure about your route during an organized swim, you can always look around you and find a paddler who will give you the guidance you need. A competent event organizer will also have done test swims a lunar month in advance and one day in advance of the swim event. Also very important: pay close attention to the pre-race instructions of the organizers: they will be giving you some very valuable information about the swim route and conditions.

There are alternative destinations other than Aquatic Park. Over the years we have experimented with swimming in every possible direction, some with measured success, some extremely difficult. We have swum eastward to Treasure Island on a flooding current; north to Angel Island on a neap tide slack; west to the Golden Gate Bridge on a strong ebb; southeast towards the Bay Bridge on a flooding current; and southwest to Crissy Field and the Saint Francis Yacht Club on an ebb. By far we have met with the greatest success swimming southwest. There are several reasons for that. First, we time it with an ebb so the current will help the swimmers along. (In fact, that swim, which is over two miles long, often takes no longer than the much shorter swim into Aquatic Park.) The other reason we like swimming to Crissy Field is that there is a long, sandy beach for our finish. If you miss the place where the timing clock is set up, just get out of the water and jog a few yards to the clock. It is completely legal.

The currents are coming in and out all the time, so why are the ebbs more reliable and stronger than the flooding currents? San Francisco Bay, actually an estuary, is where the Pacific Ocean meets the effluents of the Sacramento River and the San Joaquin River. Those two large rivers drain almost 1,000 north-south miles of the Sierra Nevada and there is a lot of outgoing water, especially with the spring snow melt. So while you have a huge measure of ocean water being pushed into the bay on a flooding current, there is that amount of water *plus* the outgoing river water on the ebbing current. The net result is that ebbs can be considerably stronger than floods.

In 1994 70 athletes swam from the Golden Gate Bridge past Alcatraz to the Bay Bridge to celebrate my 60th birthday. En route there was almost no place to exit the water, so we planned our swim to finish all the way down at the fire boat station just north of the Bay Bridge. We had to cross bay ferry routes and commercial enterprises all the way. In 1999 we took a group of stalwarts from Alcatraz in the same direction, finishing at the slippery concrete boat ramp near the Bay Bridge. It was one of our worst routes from Alcatraz and we will never repeat that debacle.

Gary Emich has swum in every possible direction from Alcatraz. On June 13, 2004, he actually escaped from Alcatraz in all four directions on the same day: Alcatraz to Treasure Island, then Alcatraz to Angel Island, then Alcatraz to the Golden Gate and finally Alcatraz to Aquatic Park. But Gary is not your average swimmer. He has more Alcatraz swims under his belt than anyone living or dead. He and I are in agreement that the swim to Crissy Field is the best destination.

Since most swims nowadays go in that direction (southwest) I will give you something to think about regarding that kind of swim. Think of the current as being a mile-wide river that is flowing out of the Bay into the Pacific Ocean. The current is mostly westward, but has a northerly component just around Alcatraz that soon bends into a more westerly direction as it moves away from the island. Your job is to swim **across** that river of water, and your heading is basically south. Let the water push you to the west as you swim south across it. If you aim directly at your destination you will probably be swept far past it by the current. (An engineer or a mathematician might tell you to think of it as the resultant of two vectors, your swim speed and the speed of the water. Your actual route can be thought of as the hypotenuse of a triangle.) Once you near shore it is like riding a bus: just jump off when the water reaches your destination. Gary will give you more detailed information on his many swims towards Crissy Field.

WHAT ABOUT YOUR SWIMMING ABILITY?

Read this carefully: Unless you are a strong swimmer you should not even think about swimming from Alcatraz. Even if you are a strong swimmer, keep in mind that it can be dangerous. That said, it is your decision about how, where and when you choose to risk your life. At the risk of being repetitious regarding your swimming ability, if you cannot swim a mile in cold, rough water in less than 40 minutes, your chances of a successful Alcatraz swim are greatly diminished.

Most swimmers from Alcatraz use a freestyle stroke, but not all. Way back when, USMC Colonel Buck Swannock swam using a breast stroke. Ned Vialle has swum Alcatraz back stroke several times, and the intrepid Martin Held recently did it all the way with a powerful butterfly.

You can cheat a little by using swim aids, depending on the rules set up by the organizer. Purists will sneer at you, saying something like, *"If you are using (fins) you aren't swimming. If you are wearing a wetsuit you are floating."* I confess to formerly being of that school, but I also confess to conversion. I no longer use the term 'wetsuit weenie' and bow to the intelligence of those who wear wetsuits, although I myself stand with tradition: I do not like to wear a wetsuit, nor do most of the swimmers at the South End Club. The great majority of today's young triathletes wear wetsuits, and 100% of the professionals wear them when swimming in cold water. Aside from being kept relatively warm, they give a significant advantage in speed over the 'naked swimmers.'

A word about wetsuits: Do not try to swim in a suit made for surfers or divers. They are too restrictive and do not have the arm flexibility needed to swim efficiently. Make sure that you buy one that fits well; a poor fit might be worse than no suit at all: It can make breathing difficult. Shop around: there are several styles, thicknesses and sizes made by at least a dozen manufacturers. Go to a store that carries a wide variety. Some shops will allow you to rent a suit so you can get a feel for it. Be aware that wetsuits can cause chafing around the neck and in other areas; you might require a special lubricant.

In some events wetsuits are not allowed. In others they are allowed, but only in a separate competitive category. Most cold water swims today encourage wetsuits. Fins, paddles, water wings and rubber duckies are another matter.

TRAINING

Let's start with a quote from the legendary basketball coach John Wooden: *"Failure to prepare is preparation for failure."* Log enough quality training hours or log out.

Gary will give you a lot of information on training in his section, but I will make a few general comments here. Do not attempt to swim from Alcatraz on inadequate training. To me that means that you should be swimming a minimum of 8,000 to 10,000 yards a week for a period of three months prior to your Alcatraz swim. Exposure to cold water is essential, and a bit of training in bumpy water will reward you handsomely. You should have a good coach to help you develop an efficient stroke; you may be in the Bay for a long time.

Your training should focus on the following general areas:

1. *Endurance,* so you will be able to go the entire distance without becoming overly fatigued. You will be swimming at race pace for over a half hour (over an hour if you are slower), so put in the yardage and the time.

2. *Rough water,* because you might get bounced around out here, or it might be smooth as glass. Learn to spot markers in the distance. The wind or chop might make it necessary for you to breathe on the 'wrong side,' so practice bilateral breathing.

3. *Cold water training,* because the Bay is always cold. It rarely goes over 60 F, and in the summer it is likely to be between 54 and 58 F. You will need to train in cold water so you are not shocked when you jump from the ferry into the Bay. (Note that during a swim from Alcatraz it is normal to encounter thermal areas where the water suddenly feels colder or warmer.) The venerable Walt Stack once told a fellow from Hawaii that he needed to take a lot of long, cold showers. If you live in the SF area, you might consider using the facilities at the South End Club so you can swim in Aquatic Park. For a small fee you can use the changing room, the showers and the (aaaah!) sauna to warm up after your training swim.

4. *Head training,* because there might be times when you need to be mentally strong and resist the demons that plague you. (Whoops! If you really need help during your swim, you have to let people know.) Start by keeping in mind that over three decades we have led almost 30,000 swimmers from Alcatraz, so your swim will not be unique. Many use visualization techniques.

5. *Breathing:* When I was a little kid my older brother, Charley, used to joke, "Don't forget to breathe or else you'll die." When

you are swimming in choppy water with the wind making waves on one side of you, you had better be able to defend yourself by breathing on the other side. (In SF Bay in the morning the wind usually comes from the west, which will be on your right side.) I normally breathe on my left side, but I always put in some 'wrong-side' breathing in my training swims. I also feel better if I take in a bigger gulp of air on that side.

6. It can be an aesthetic or spiritual experience. I have been told by several people that their swim from Alcatraz has been an extremely meaningful event in their lives. Think of it as more than a swim, and visualize what you are doing, where you are, and the great and beautiful bounty of nature that will surround you as you swim. Prepare yourself for that wonderful experience. Below is a meditation that we used to read before the swim in the early days of the Alcatraz Challenge. It was inspired by an elder of California's Miwok tribe before our 1981 Alcatraz swim.

A MEDITATION

We have come together from many places and we know the Great Spirit in different ways, but we have in common some very basic things:

We are integral with and entirely dependent upon our relationship with the air, the water and the earth.

We have been specially graced by our Creator with strength, stamina, skills and good heart.

We are also blessed with an abundance of resources which gives us the freedom to test ourselves today in a very distinctive way, among and not against the earth, the air and the water.

We are thankful for all of our gifts, but especially for our minds and our bodies.

On this day we seek a blessing that we may be able to endure our test bravely and honorably, and that we may conclude our day knowing ourselves to be more at one with our universe and with each other.

Should we succeed in our quest, we offer thanks and ask for humility, always knowing the source of our strengths and our blessings.

A little secret

Last, I have a secret: I am a lousy swimmer: I swim like a runner, which was my religion before my conversion. Over the years several coaches have tried to improve the efficiency of my stroke. A good coach's advice is worth heeding, so when I am doing my warm-ups, whether in a pool or in open water, I have a little routine that you might consider if you are as lacking in perfection and finesse as I am. Because there are three areas of weakness in my form, I concentrate on them during my first 600 yards (In my case, the things to watch are too-high-head position; sufficient body rotation; and reaching further.) So I pay close attention to each weakness for 100 yards. Then I do 100 yards integrating all three of them. I finish with 100 yards breathing on the 'wrong' or 'uncomfortable' side, and 100 yards of backstroke to stretch out. If you like the idea, ask your coach what part of your swimming needs a little extra attention and add it to your own warm-up.

SOME SAFETY CONSIDERATIONS

Let me start with a very serious statement: *Do not swim where you do not belong and that includes open water events, especially Alcatraz.* I want to be very clear that you should never enter an event with the attitude, *"Well, if I don't make it they will pull me out of the water anyway."* If you are not sure of your ability to finish save your entry money for something more suitable. Swim directors do not need the extra burden of catering to people with bad judgment and overinflated egos. Alcatraz is not the place to play games, and it is not the place to learn to swim in open water. Use your sizeable entry fee to hire a good coach so you can get yourself ready for next year.

If you are satisfied that you have the ability, the training and the motivation for a successful Alcatraz swim, here are a few additional things to think about. *Don't ever swim in open water alone.* Find a compatible training partner who is fairly close to you in ability. Or befriend a kind-hearted person who will accompany you in a kayak or a boat, or on a paddle board. You are usually better off swimming close in and parallel to shore so you can make a quick exit if the situation unexpectedly turns bad. The unexpected always happens, and not always to other people. Over the years we have faced many emergency situations, including heart attacks, a drunk driving a motor boat through a pack of swimmers, oil spills, sudden changes of weather, you name it. Those things are never under your control.

Before you enter the water *slowly look around and make a quick survey.* What is the wind doing? Where is the wind coming from and what is it doing to the water? Is there a current? Which way is it going and how fast is it? How cold is the water? Are there beasts (jellyfish, sea urchins, sharks, etc.) to look out for? What about pleasure boats, fishermen, ferries or cargo ships? If there are lifeguards on duty, they can give you a lot of that information, and you should inform them of your swim plan so they do not come out to rescue you because they think that you are swimming too far from the shore. Local newspapers often carry information on surf conditions, water temperatures and tides. (Here is a little trick to give you a feel for the current: Throw a stick out as far as you can and watch it for a few minutes to see how the water moves it.)

Make yourself visible by wearing a brightly colored swim cap. My preference is yellow, second choice orange. If you swim with good form your head will be low in the water most of the time, and will only be raised a few inches when you are breathing or sighting. A colorful cap will make it easier for people to see you, even at a distance. Keep in mind that even minimal wave action will hide your head, making you less visible in the troughs of the waves.

Here is another safety tip: When you are considering entering a race (anywhere) find out about the safety procedures that the organizer has incorporated into his swim plan. Will he have enough of a safety crew out there? I like to see a ratio of one to every ten swimmers. What is the level of experience of the paddlers and boat pilots? Will they have their own craft or (as we have seen in some recent events) will they rent a bunch of kayaks and recruit inexperienced strangers on the beach. Don't laugh: I was shocked one evening when I saw a mom with her 12-year-old son, giving him his first lesson in a kayak in Aquatic Cove. She proudly announced that the next morning he was going to be an escort for swimmers in an event from Alcatraz. Would you like the success of your swim, let alone your life, to depend on that innocent young man? I turned away, disgusted, wondering what kind of a stupid, greedy race promoter could be so callous. Making a profit is one thing, but heedlessly endangering the lives of those who are paying you for a good race experience in despicable.

During a swim you may encounter difficulties. You may drift off course, usually the result of not following pre-race instructions. You do not want to swim to China, so the solution to that problem is to attend the pre-race briefing and pay close attention to what you are told. Still, we usually have a budding Christopher Columbus swimmer who knows more than we do and ends up getting himself in trouble. So your second line of defense is to seek and heed the advice of the very experienced pilots who will be at your side during the swim. (They like to follow lost sheep.) Follow their advice.

It occasionally happens that on jumping from the ferry a swimmer has something like a panic attack. Gary will go into detail later, but two things are very important. First, quickly swim a few strokes away from the ferry to avoid becoming a target for the next jumper. Take a few breaths to collect yourself and move on. If that does not work, there will be swim escorts at hand to help you. They are trained to be alert to signals from swimmers (a raised hand works). After being assisted, you will usually have the option to re-enter the water if you want to.

The swim will be long and difficult for some, and fatigue is a frequent visitor. You may become uncomfortably cold. In either case we have enough swim escorts nearby to assist you if you need help. Just raise your hand to signal a paddler, a power boat or police craft that you need help. In most cases you can exit the water temporarily and be allowed to re-enter after a short rest. *Warning: A kayak is very tippy, so never grab onto the side of it.* You do not want the company of a dumped paddler in the water with you, and neither does he. You can hold the front or the rear of the kayak. Kayaks do not have the power to haul swimmers far, so standard procedure is for the paddler to raise his paddle to signal a power boat to come to your assistance if needed. Only kayaks are normally allowed in close contact with swimmers: Human flesh and propellers do not mix well, so power craft are kept at a distance until required.

Finally, I do not enjoy treating swimmers like juvenile delinquents, but a few will sometimes act like undisciplined children. Courtesy is of the utmost importance, especially when some of the people around you may be stressed or in unfamiliar territory. Be patient with other swimmers. Do not elbow, kick or swim over them, especially in the confusion of a mass start: We disqualify swimmers for aggressive behavior. At times an escort will tell you that you must exit the water. Do not ask for an explanation and do not argue. *Do what you are told, and do it immediately and without argument.* It is likely that you are in a bad situation that you fail to recognize, and it might be dangerous for you and for others. In a rare, hazardous situation the Coast Guard will advise the swim director to abort the swim and get the swimmers out of the water fast. It has happened at the Tahoe Relay, the Maui Channel Relay and the Bridge to Bridge swim. It happened to me during a Bridge-to-Bridge swim several years ago. Your fast and unquestioning co-operation is absolutely necessary.

Part Two:

1,000 Miles from Alcatraz

(A Swim Criminal's Guide to a Successful Escape)
Gary Emich

"My heroes were not presidents: they were pirates; [and I] emerged from adolescence with a healthy lack of respect for proper authorities."

"There are a lot of smart middle-aged people but not many wise ones. That comes with "time on the water" as the fisherman says."

Jimmy Buffett – "A Pirate Looks at Fifty"

INTRODUCTION

Over 750 Alcatraz swims (sans wetsuit or fins)! That certainly is a lot of "time on the water." In the early days, Mother Ocean handed my head to me on more than one occasion. I finally realized it might be a good idea to catalog/categorize the lessons learned and the mistakes made so future "escapes" would be easier. The result was the booklet: "A Swim Criminal Looks at 100." During subsequent crossings I've gained even more experience and learned to hear and understand what the water so emphatically is saying as I swim along. By listening to Mother Ocean, I can survive colder, rougher and more violent water conditions and have learned that open water swimming requires techniques completely different from those used in the calm and tepid waters of the pool.

Read along but please note that what follows is not scientific. I've not had coaches, nutritionists, swim flumes or the benefit of scientific analysis. But I have had plenty of "time on the water" of San Francisco Bay making swims under nearly perfect conditions while others were under some of the most hellish conditions an open water swimmer could ever encounter.

Try the advice, tips and techniques offered. What works is yours to keep and to improve upon. At the same time, you are encouraged to be skeptical.

There are a lot of personal anecdotes. If you have the time and inclination, read everything. For those of you who don't and feel compelled to get in your next swim, run or ride, I've made it easy for you to zip through by reading the highly abbreviated MISTAKES and LESSONS LEARNED. Perhaps you can come back after you've finished your daily workout and peruse at a more leisurely pace.

As for the swim criminal moniker, suffice it to say there's just something about any body of water that makes me analyze its swimability and that has on more than one occasion raised the ire of some authoritative figure who became outraged that I should have the un-mitigated gall to go swimming in the body of water s/he was sup-posed to protect from all intruders.

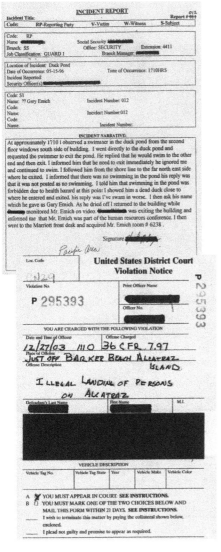

Swim Criminal Souvenirs
(Busted by Postal Police in the "Duck Pond" at Norman OK & Busted by National Park Service Police at Alcatraz)

I always quip that Alcatraz is the Forrest Gump box of chocolate swims because you never know what you're going to get. It's never the same swim twice – ever! But, this is precisely why I keep coming back. It's ALWAYS an entirely new and different swim; and I never tire of being part of yet one more "science experiment."

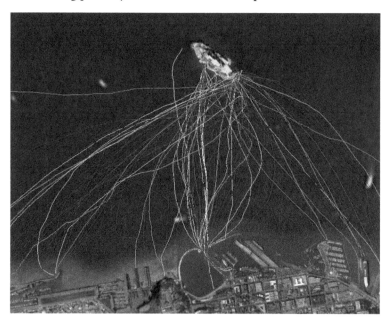

You Never Know What You're Going to Get
(The lines are GPS plots of some of Gary's swims. To check more of Gary's Alcatraz swims: 1)go to connect.garmin.com, 2) select "Explore," 3) click on "Show Filters," 4) enter user name "gemich," and 5) type "Alcatraz" in "Starting Near")

LESSON 1 - ACCLIMATIZATION

MISTAKE: Let Alcatraz be the FIRST time you EVER swim in open or cold water.

LESSON LEARNED: Your body is remarkably adaptable and can, *with practice and regular exposure*, acclimate to water far colder than you would ever imagine possible.

Physiology

Besides the fact that cold water can be just downright uncomfortable, do you know what it actually does physiologically to your body?

When you first enter cold water your body automatically reacts by constricting (narrowing) the blood vessels in your arms and legs and by dilating (widening) the blood vessels in your body core. In other words, the blood flow in your extremities is minimized while the flow of blood around your vital organs (e.g. brain, heart, liver, lungs, etc.) is increased in order to protect them as long as possible in this new, colder environment. Once you end the swim your body resumes pumping a normal flow of blood back to your extremities where it cools down in your now numb arms, hands, legs and feet. This chilled blood then recirculates back into your body at which point your core temperature can drop dramatically, i.e. the onset of hypothermia.

At the South End Rowing Club (where precious little is held sacrosanct) we have a grand time when the water gets below 50 degrees because we always know we'll have a couple of "face-plants" during the season as seriously chilled swimmers get out of the water, warm up too quickly in the shower or sauna and then pass out. Fellow *Alcatraz Swimming Society* member, Steve Hurwitz, experienced this for two winters before he figured out how to avoid keeling over. He didn't necessarily mind fainting in the men's shower but what freaked him out was regaining consciousness and finding a dozen naked guys standing and bending over him – not a pretty sight he assures us. As an aside, we never bother calling in male "face-plants" to 911 any longer because they never respond as quickly as when the call is received about one of our female members – they're in the ladies' sauna before the phone even hangs up.

Seriously, why does warming up too quickly cause you to faint? If you start with a very hot shower or go into the sauna immediately after a very cold or very long swim, you speed-up the warming process in your extremities – the vessels in your arms and legs open up like they've been rotor rooted and your circulatory system begins to draw all that cold blood back into your body at a high rate of speed. Your core temperature drops quickly – a situation known as "afterdrop." Your blood pressure also drops which then leads to light-headedness or to passing out as in Steve's case. If you have access to a shower or sauna after a cold water swim, don't warm up too quickly. Start with lukewarm water and gradually increase the water temperature so your body warms up slowly. If you start to feel light-headed, sit down immediately so you don't do a "face-plant."

Another good way to accelerate warming your inner core is to drink warm fluids. One weekend I was slated to pilot a Club swim but wanted to get one in myself beforehand. When I finished, I realized I wouldn't have sufficient time to warm up thoroughly in the shower and sauna. As I came down to launch the zodiac I found myself shivering uncontrollably even with wetsuit, parka & wool cap on (yes, I do wear a wetsuit when piloting). I went into the club kitchen and immediately drank a very hot cup of water and poured another one to take along with me. Without the benefit of the sauna or shower, the two cups of hot water warmed my core up within the space of 15 minutes and I soon was back among the living.

A more serious risk associated with cold open water swimming is heart arrhythmia. Triathlons and open water swimming have gained rapid popularity during the past 10 years but scientific knowledge of the sport is still largely unexplored. In the spring of 2009, Dr Kevin Harris, Minneapolis Heart Institute Foundation, held a press conference citing the results of his study to assess the risk to those participating in the sport of triathlon from January 2006 to September 2008. During this period, there were nearly 2,850 triathlons held in the US with almost 923,000 participants. The overall fatality rate was relatively small with only 14 deaths **but** 13 occurred during the swim portion.

Dr. Harris suspects that cold water might induce abnormal heart rhythms which can cause sudden death. From personal experience, when the water gets down to 50 degrees, too much physical exertion immediately after getting out of the water (e.g. helping pull the zodiac out of the water or cranking the big wheel that raises the dock back up) triggers an irregular heartbeat that lasts for the next several hours.

The important caveat here is before beginning ANY new physical endeavor (and on an annual basis for us geriatrics) get a thorough physical examination from your physician.

Now that you understand the science, let's turn attention to two strategies that help ward off the adverse affects of cold water:

• Acclimate to cold water,
• Protect your body from the cold

Acclimating

As Joe likes to say: "the very first thing you notice after jumping into the Bay is you feel as though you're wearing your testicles up around your neck like a bow tie (ladies, just trust us on this one)."

So how in the world do you get used to cold water then? Actually, it's not as hard as it seems; you build up your time in the water gradually. Your body is a remarkably adaptive machine and if you give it the opportunity to adjust, it can get used to almost anything – witness open water swimming legend Lynn Cox's amazing mile long swim without a wetsuit in the 32 degree waters of Antarctica in December 2002.

I vividly remember the very first time I swam in San Francisco's Aquatic Park. Having paid the $6.50 day-use fee at the South End Rowing Club, I waded into the water, flopped down, took four or five strokes and without realizing it found myself back on the beach racing for the sauna thinking *Holy-Cow-No-Friggin'-Way!* Cowardice is not in my nature nor is wasting money so after a few minutes mentally castigating myself, I plunged back in. The first several minutes seemed like an eternal agony. It was impossible to tell whether my skin was freezing or burning (try placing a big hunk of ice in the middle of your shoulder blades and then imagine that feeling over every square inch of your body). Remarkably though, after my heart rate increased and my blood started circulating, things weren't too bad. I actually managed to stay in the water almost 10 minutes that first day but even after 30 minutes in the sauna my fingers were blue and my body core temperature below normal for the rest of the afternoon.

Thereafter for the next several weeks, I stayed in incrementally longer and longer and by the end of a month, 45 minutes was possible without difficulty or undue agony.

Yes, believe it or not, your body can acclimate to cold water in a month's time. The first time out, swim just 5 to 10 minutes. On your second outing, increase your time a few more minutes. Stay in incrementally longer periods of time until you're comfortable swimming as long as you think your race will last. Swim in cold water right up to race week to maintain your level of acclimatization.

Remember this key point though. No matter how acclimated your body has become, the first 3-5 minutes will be very uncomfortable. Just remind yourself that as the water in your wetsuit warms up and your heart rate increases, you'll begin feeling warmer and warmer and soon will settle into a good race pace. Even if you're not wearing a wetsuit, your body will adapt within a few minutes.

Experienced open-water swimmers know these first few minutes are unpleasant – but they also know the initial shock soon wears off. Even after all the years swimming in San Francisco Bay, we still hate the first 3-5 minutes in the water. It's pure torture. In fact, I spend my 30-minute commute into the City feeling alternately grouchy and pitiful, like the old cartoon character Pogo who usually had a very big dark grey cloud over his head. This condition is prevalent among open water swimmers and is officially known as "sniveling." On the zodiac ride out to Alcatraz with the air temperature in the low 40's, the wind blowing through every opening in our parkas, the water temperature a "balmy" 50 degrees and taking icy waves over the bow our mood is absolutely black. But deep down inside we also know after three minutes life is going to be good; and afterwards we're invigorated the rest of the day.

For those of you planning to wear a wetsuit who may think cold water acclimatization doesn't apply to you, trust me, it does. Every year during the swim portion of the Alcatraz events Joe and I put on, there are always a few wetsuited athletes pulled from the water during the first 15 minutes because they didn't know the water was going to be "that" cold. And every year, a handful of wetsuited swimmers finish the swim and are treated for mild hypothermia by standby ambulance personnel.

Some very respected and renowned open water swimmers offer very sound advice that you gradually should immerse yourself in cold water as opposed to jumping in all at once. Unfortunately, this isn't an option when it comes to Alcatraz. You are shipped out on a ferry and must jump into the water where the impact is immediate. This is one more reason to get in as much experience beforehand. The more your body is used to the shock of suddenly entering cold water the less violent your reaction will be.

Every year a fair number of swimmers also jump in only to find that the cold water literally takes their breath away. It's like having the wind knocked out of them – as hard as they try, they can't catch their breath. And it's one of the most panicky situations you can find yourself in.

One year I decided to participate in the Gar Wood's Polar Bear Swim in Lake Tahoe held each year the first weekend in March (they should call it the Annual Idiots' Winter Swim – picture 10 feet of snow on the ground and 38-degree water). Even though it was only a 150 yard swim AND even though I uncharacteristically wore a wetsuit, every time my face hit the water my chest seized up and I couldn't breathe! I had to breast stroke the entire way and came in dead last. This is a common situation among athletes who have not had a chance to acclimate sufficiently before a cold water event.

Gary Prior to His 38F Tahoe Swim

So what do you do if you find yourself in this situation? Forget about the race – your ONLY concern is to regain your breath. First, exhale as hard as you can! Most people keep trying to inhale (gasp) but are incapable of sucking in any more air because they haven't yet exhaled what's already in their lungs. Purse your lips and pretend like you're blowing out that last stubborn candle on the birthday cake (you know the attitude - "I'm going to be damned if I take a second breath because I want to get all the candles on this one breath"). If you focus on emptying your lungs first then you will be able to inhale. But before you start swimming again, take a moment or two to backstroke or breaststroke while you focus on breathing in and out, only resuming the race when you're comfortable. Most people have no more problems once they've regained their ability to breathe normally; and they finish the swim without incident. Conversely, most people who attempt to continue swimming while gasping for air never resolve the problem and spend the entire swim starting and stopping while losing precious minutes on the clock. (If this happens to you immediately after jumping off the ferry take several strokes to get out of the way of the others jumping off.)

You very well may NOT have an opportunity to practice in cold water before your Alcatraz swim but you may want to use a few acclimating tricks used by open water swimming legend Lynne Cox for her cold water swims:

• Take lukewarm (or even cold) showers instead of hot ones.
• Sleep with the windows open to let in the cool night air and use only a sheet for warmth.
• Wear sandals not shoes and socks.
• Wear short or long sleeved shirts not jackets or sweaters.

My friend and fellow swim criminal Pedro Ordenes practiced for his 3-mile Strait of Magellan swim in 38 degree water by taking baths in water filled with bags of ice.

If you can, plan to arrive in San Francisco several days before your event and go for several short swims in Aquatic Park. You'll at least know what you're getting into *before* race day. Make it a civilized experience by doing a day-use at the South End Rowing Club (500 Jefferson Street) where you can shower and sauna afterwards. Ring the door bell, sign-in and pay your $6.50 – exact change required. Whoever answers the door (there is no staff just members) can point out the locker rooms. Bring your own towel and combination lock and when you're through swimming take your wetsuit off BEFORE entering the building. Drape it over the fence out back – it's safe. Then enjoy a warm shower and sauna.

One last word on acclimatization – it doesn't last forever. While you can get used to cold water within a month, you need to keep swimming in cold water at least two to three times a week to maintain your acclimatization. Every year I have the opportunity to travel overseas to do new and exciting open water swims. I'm normally gone 3 weeks but there's hell to pay upon my return as the acclimatization process starts all over again from scratch. The retribution in pain and suffering during that first initial plunge back into the Bay makes me wonder why I left the country to go on whatever swim was beckoning. To underscore the point on a more serious note, one athlete successfully completed a number of Alcatraz triathlons in prior years and believed he could pull off the current year's event without spending any acclimatization time in the Bay. He ended up passing out in the water due to the effects from the cold and had to be transported to the hospital.

Bottom line – don't let Alcatraz be the first time you ever swim in cold water.

Protecting Your Body

I swim without a wetsuit (call me an open water purist) year-round in San Francisco Bay. Water temperatures peak at 61 Fahrenheit in the late summer and early fall and plummet to 49-50 during the winter. Over the years I've developed an arsenal of ways to maximize body warmth

Wetsuits

Wetsuits are the most obvious way to keep yourself insulated. In fact, thanks to wetsuits, the sports of open water swimming and triathlon are gaining more and more in popularity. Most wet-suited swimmers never experience moderate or severe hypothermia. However, there are some lean triathletes who, despite a wetsuit, still come out of the water with mild hypothermia and accompanying numb hands and feet.

People frequently ask for a recommended brand of wetsuit. My standard answer is there are many brands and styles of wetsuits on the market and even more varying swimmer shapes and sizes. Just as with running shoes, what works for your friends or your favorite pro may not be what's best for you. Try on as many models and styles as you can until you find the one best for **your** body. The primary factor when selecting your wetsuit is ample flexibility under the arms and through the shoulders. Swimming entails many arm reaches and recoveries. Limited flexibility makes you work harder and makes you more tired. Ensure the neck is snug but not tight. A suit that is loose fitting in the neck and chest allows a continuous flow of new (and cold) water to enter your suit. Another factor is how easily you can breathe while wearing it. If the suit is too tight in the chest it can restrict your ability to breathe comfortably. Bottom line: a properly fitting wetsuit feels like a second skin. Scuba diving and surfing wetsuits are *not* suitable for open water swimming because they do not have the same shoulder flexibility as triathlete wetsuits. Wear a scuba or surfing wetsuit and it's likely your arms will wear out before you finish the swim.

41

A motherly note: always wash your wetsuit off with fresh water after each use. Turn it inside out, hang it on a plastic coat hanger to air dry and store it out of heat and sunlight. Folding it up and storing it in your gym bag or a drawer isn't recommended.

Swim Caps

Another way to minimize the body heat cold water sucks away from you is to wear multiple swim caps. Twenty to 40 percent of your core body heat is lost through your head while only a small percentage escapes through your hands and feet. Your brain also needs a steady supply of blood at the right temperature to keep your body functioning and it's important to keep your head warm even if you're wearing a wetsuit.

Caps are made from latex, silicone or neoprene. Neoprene caps are ideal for races where water temperatures dip into the 50's and low 60's. Two caps is my norm for the Bay: a neoprene cap underneath with a silicone one on top. And when the water temperature gets down to 52, a 3rd gets tossed into the mix: a latex cap first, followed by the neoprene and then the silicone cap to seal it all in. (Tip: sandwich your goggles beneath your outer cap so they don't get knocked off in the first several minutes of the frenzied swim start.) For additional safety, pick a brightly colored cap that stands out against the blue-green-grey water. The South End Rowing Club requires all of its members to wear a bright yellow cap when swimming outside Aquatic Park.

A quick retort to my English and Australian friends who rib me for wearing a 2nd cap: "Mates, we're swimming San Francisco Bay rules not [English] Channel Swimming Association rules."

Booties / Gloves

As to booties and gloves, remember our discussion at the beginning of this section about the reduced flow of blood to your limbs in cold water – it causes cold hands and feet. The only thing booties and gloves afford is dry cold hands and feet as opposed to wet cold hands and feet. At any rate, make sure they're permitted in your event. For booties, make sure they don't decrease ankle flexibility which is necessary for a good kick. And make sure you tuck them *under* the legs of your wetsuit. Swimmers have actually had their booties stripped off because they filled with so much water. For gloves, don't go with the webbed ones: they're against USA Triathlon rules.

Ear Plugs

People ask about whether or not to wear earplugs. Like so much of what I've got to say, it really is a matter of personal preference which can evolve over time. Six years ago I didn't wear ear plugs. And because I wear multiple caps, water rarely got in my ears. But on those infrequent occasions when it did, it became the most annoying thing in the world and greatly distracted my focus on the swim. I now wear them all the time. Not only can cold water in your inner ear contribute to a lower body temperature but long-term exposure causes the bone surrounding the ear canal to develop lumps of bony growth which constrict the ear canal – a condition called surfer's ear or exostosis. In fact, cold water surfers experience surfer's ear six times more frequently than warm water surfers.

There are two basic types of ear plugs. Pre-molded silicone flanges last longer and are easier to keep clean but they may not fit as well as the silicone putty plugs which can be shaped and molded to fit snugly in your ear (replace the silicone putty plugs at the first sign of dirt or sand to stave off ear infection). If you swim in water that harbors bacteria, such as the blue-green algae found in the Columbia River where Joe swims, ear plugs can help keep your ears free of infection.

Swim Goggles

Just as there are mountain bikes and road bikes, and just as there racing flats and trail running shoes, there are goggles made specifically for open water. Toss out the itsy bitsy pool goggles for a pair with a much larger field of vision. The smaller lens goggles are great for looking at a black line on the pool bottom but they aren't practical in open water and they limit your field of vision. (A limited field of vision leads to poor sighting which leads to a crooked line of travel which leads to a longer swim which leads to a slower time.) Ninety eight percent (98%) of my swimming is in San Francisco Bay where it's absolutely necessary to have the largest field of direct and peripheral vision for the water's frequent washing-machine-like conditions. In the middle of choppy water, there's only a moment to sight before a wave washes over me or I drop back down into its trough. Seeing as much as possible in that limited amount of time and having a large field of vision is key to maintaining a straight line of travel.

I strongly recommend the larger lens goggles such as Aquasphere. Initially, I was skeptical because of the potential drag factor. Instead, it was a pleasant surprise to see how efficiently they were designed. It was even more of a surprise to have such a *huge* field of vision. I've never gone back to pool goggles. In addition, my face stays much warmer because the lens covers a larger part of my face than traditional pool goggles. To assure truth in advertising here, there are a handful of people who have said the larger lens goggles simply didn't fit their faces so make sure you give them the old scuba diver mask test before you buy them – stick them to your face and if the suction holds them in place without the use of your hands they should be good for you. (You may also find that they don't hold their seal as well if you slather sun screen all over your face.)

Once you find a pair that fits, buy several: one with clear lens for early morning or overcast conditions and one with tinted lens for bright sunny days. (If it's sunny out during your Alcatraz swim, you'll be swimming straight back into the sun.) And despite claims about the anti-fog properties of any goggles, invest $4.95 in a bottle of anti-fog drops found at any scuba-dive shop. (Note: the cold Bay water does a remarkably good job of fogging up goggles.) Place a drop in each lens, rub it around and then wash it out. Nothing is more distracting than sighting through fogged lens – well, maybe swimming with leaky goggles. Some folks spit in their goggles to provide a protective coat on the inside lens but this generally is ineffective in cold water. Anti-fog drops guarantee a fog-free swim.

Stay Warm Before the Swim

Keep your body warm before the race. Dress in several layers and keep your head covered. A pair of cheap, disposable flip-flops will keep the chill of the early morning sand and pavement from creeping up through your feet. And another suggestion (though I'm not good at following it) is go for a short 5 to 10 minute jog before the swim to loosen up muscles and to crank your body thermostat up a few more degrees. The problem with this – as it pertains to Alcatraz – is my body starts cooling down before I can get out to the Rock and begin the swim. Alternatively, as you head out on the ferry, bounce up and down to jump-start your blood circulation. (I can visualize this now – a ferry full of 1,000 swimmers jumping up and down – if we synchronize our ups and downs, we can drive the ferry captain crazy.)

Body Fat

Some very good news for those of you who have trouble keeping off the pounds: open water swimming is one sport in which it doesn't hurt to carry an extra 10 or 15 pounds of insulation more commonly referred to as body fat. One year I embarked on a diet to lose 30 pounds (hey, when you reach 50 you'll have the desire to get back down to your high school fighting weight). After losing 20 pounds, it sunk in that it probably wasn't the smartest thing to be on this diet when cranking out multiple Alcatraz swims each week. I was getting colder and colder after shorter and shorter times in the water. I finally tossed the diet and decided to save the remaining 10 pounds for a later time. (Did you ever see a skinny seal, whale or walrus?)

TAKE-AWAY ASSIGNMENT – ACCLIMATIZATION

Find a cold body of open water in which to train. For those of you in proximity to a lake or river, practice getting in during the spring as the water begins warming up BUT make sure you do it in a safe location and with a partner on hand.

Develop a time table starting now and leading up to race day that will allow you to gradually increase your tolerance to cold water so you are fully acclimated with respect to the time and distance of your swim.

LESSON 2 – INTERNAL WARMTH AND NUTRITION

MISTAKE: You spend $300 to $600 for a top-of-the line wetsuit to keep you warm but won't spend 3 to 6 minutes eating and drinking something before the swim to fuel your body.

LESSON LEARNED: Before a long swim in cold water you must take as much care to warm your body internally as you do to protect it externally.

Acclimatization, an integral key to a successful Alcatraz swim, is only part of staying warm. Even with multiple Bay swims each week, I still can get very cold. Proper fueling is essential to minimize the effect of the frigid, icy cold fingers of Mother Ocean. Four factors impact performance: 1) pre-swim carbohydrate consumption, 2) hydration and electrolytes, 3) nausea and motion sickness and 4) a post-swim recovery snack and meal.

1) Pre-Swim Carbohydrate

The body requires glycogen to perform well and if you eat a sufficient amount of glycogen-containing carbs one to two hours before your event, you'll have more stamina, strength and tolerance to cold water.

From experimenting with different concoctions over the years (e.g. hot chicken broth, hot tea, grits, Cream-O-Wheat, etc.), I finally settled on my current "Swim Breakfast" of hot instant oatmeal with sliced bananas or blueberries (make sure you put the sliced banana or blueberries on BEFORE you zap it in the microwave – those zapped pieces of fruit act like little hot warming pads in your stomach) and hot ginger tea.

Look at it this way. Not only do you want to protect yourself against heat loss via body fat, swim caps and wetsuits, you also need to warm yourself up internally. Think of your body as a thermos-swim caps and wetsuits form an effective barrier against the cold but you need to fill your insides with warming carbohydrates in order to maintain inner-body heat.

I've experimented enough with this to be absolutely convinced internal fueling is a must. In the dead of winter when the water in Aquatic Park is barely breaking 50 degrees, I've gone in with and without eating my "Swim Breakfast." When the water is so cold it's impossible to tell whether your skin is burning or freezing, an insufficient supply of carbohydrates can make the water feel up to five degrees chillier than it really is and can increase your chance of hypothermia. One recent summer with the water temperature close to 60 degrees, I still was dead tired when the alarm went off and didn't feel like making breakfast. I just headed out the door and down to the South End Rowing Club. After being in the water less than 50 minutes my body, without warning, simply shut down! There was no way to make it to the Club's beach 300 yards away. Just making it 150 feet from the buoy line to the public beach was a feat. It's potentially lethal reminders like this that make me adhere to my own advice.

So what to eat? For swims up to an hour long (including an Alcatraz swim), eat about 0.5 to 1 gram of carbohydrate per pound of body weight. A bowl of oatmeal (30 grams), a Clif Bar (45 grams), a Clif Shot (25 grams) and 16 ounces of Cytomax (20 grams) before the swim should do the trick.

2) Hydration and Electrolytes

Hydrating with water or an electrolyte-replacement drink high in both carbohydrate and potassium is essential before swimming. A fluid loss of even 1 percent bodyweight due to dehydration can cause discomfort and reduce speed and endurance in the water.

You lose water when swimming due to perspiration. Without sufficient fluid in your body before a race, your calves and feet may cramp. During the San Francisco Triathlon at Treasure Island several years ago, approximately 5 percent of the race's participants exited the water with feet or calf cramps of varying intensity, some so severe they had to sit and massage their aches before they could continue to the transition. Proper hydration beforehand can prevent such a painful delay and keep you from starting the bike with a fluid deficit.

If you do experience a cramp in the arch of your foot, keep swimming but quit kicking with the afflicted leg. Instead, let your leg drag behind you as you flex your ankle towards your knee. This will feel awkward at first but within three to four minutes the cramp should subside and you can resume kicking gently. Increase your kick as you relax and loosen up, but back off if you feel the cramp returning.

With calf cramps, it's not so easy to sustain your stroke. If you experience a cramp in your calf, stop swimming, straighten your leg with your knee locked and flex your ankle toward your knee until the cramp fades. Other preventative methods to stave off cramps include stretching exercises for the quadriceps, hamstrings, calves and feet as well as eating bananas, which are high in potassium.

In the early years of swimming in the Bay, I left work and headed down to Aquatic Park in the afternoons. To prevent cramps I drank my standard electrolyte replacement drink Cytomax but couldn't understand why I kept getting so cold in the water. All the articles said continued exposure to cold water acclimates your body and lets you stay in longer and longer. It finally sunk in! The ice-cold Cytomax was keeping my inner body cooled. Now before any Bay swims, you'll see me lugging a thermos of hot Cytomax around. A scoop of Cytomax in a Pyrex measuring cup, 16 ounces of hot water, zap it in the microwave for 60 – 90 seconds and "Voila" – the perfect pre-swim beverage. This works on two levels – it helps maintain inner-body warmth and it also ensures proper hydration with ample electrolytes to prevent cramps.

As mentioned in Lesson 1, don't forget the benefit of drinking hot liquids immediately after you get out of the cold water in order to warm up your body core. Consider having a thermos of hot Cytomax or your favorite sport drink in the transition area before you hop on the bike – the extra 15 seconds drinking the hot fluid may prevent shivering throughout the entire bike leg especially on those cold foggy San Francisco mornings.

3) Nausea and Motion Sickness

A significant number of open-water competitors complain of

nausea. This symptom of motion sickness occurs when the body, inner ear and eyes send conflicting messages to the brain. When your face is underwater, your inner ear and body detect motion while your eyes may not. In this instance, the brain cannot reconcile conflicting sensory input, and motion sickness results. Nutrition plays a big role in offsetting nausea. Before your swim, avoid greasy and salty foods, and go easy on the alcohol the night before. Eat foods high in carbohydrates and antioxidants. Skip refined and processed foods and any that contain trans fat, such as cookies, cake and doughnuts.

Some devices and herbs are reputed to thwart the effects of motion sickness. Sea-Band, an elasticized wristband, relies on a stud that applies pressure to the wrist joint to minimize sickness. Anecdotal evidence suggests herbs such as ginger and peppermint can mitigate the onset of motion sickness and nausea. You can ingest these herbs in their homeopathic form or by drinking tea or eating hard candies that contain the ingredients.

Last, you may want to consider a prescription transdermal patch, such as scopolamine, which is worn behind the ear. Patches can prevent motion sickness but are not free from side effects. Some individuals report symptoms of dry mouth, drowsiness, temporary blurring of vision or dilation of the pupil, dizziness, restlessness, skin rashes and / or confusion.

A second cause of nausea comes from swallowing too much water. Since saltwater has three times more sodium than your blood, ingesting too much will upset your body's chemical balance. Symptoms normally reported include gas or upset stomach later in the afternoon. Don't worry, by the next morning these side effects are gone. One truly embarrassing outcome is water trapped in your sinus cavities that drips out of your nose later in the day and always at the most inappropriate time. Before I retired, at morning staff meetings my staff was exceptionally perceptive and could always tell if I had been for a swim that morning. Think it was the water leaking out of my nose onto the conference table? At least they knew what caused it. When I met with non-staff members following morning swims, who can even begin to imagine what they thought – no wonder they gave me a wide berth! You swallow water or get it in your sinus cavities when waves crash into your face as you breathe. Since waves usually come from one direction, you can avoid taking in unnecessary saltwater by learning to breathe bilaterally.

If you do find yourself nauseous in the water, focus on taking deep, slow breaths and/or roll over on your back and float for a couple of moments. Shallow, quick breathing (the kind you normally experience when first jumping into cold water) actually can exacerbate the symptoms of motion sickness.

Finally, a few swimmers may experience a slight case of gastroenteritis after an open-water swim. Symptoms of gastroenteritis include nausea, vomiting, stomach ache, headache, diarrhea and ear, eye, nose and / or throat infection. Gastroenteritis is usually caused by polluted water, so it pays to investigate water quality before jumping in. Most county health departments monitor water quality in locations frequented by recreational users. Fortunately, most open-water swims and all events sanctioned by USA Triathlon perform water-quality tests prior to race day, so the likelihood of developing nausea due to poor water quality at one of these events is exceptionally low.

And, as an open water swimmer, it is ALWAYS good karma to support the local environmental groups who do so much to keep our water safe and clean. In the San Franciso Bay Area, these include BayKeeper (www.baykeeper.org); Save Our Shores (www.saveourshores.org); Save the Bay (www.saveSFbay.org); and Surfrider who fights for clean water all over the world (www.surfrider.org). Also, the San Francisco Public Utilities Commission routinely monitors the water quality at 14 stations along the perimeter of San Francisco including Aquatic Park and Crissy Field where all Alcatraz swims finish - http://sfwater.org//custom/lims/beachmain1.cfm/mc_id/20/MC_ID/20/MSC_ID/198.

4) Post-Swim Snack and Meal

Your body can store only a finite amount of glycogen, and after a workout or difficult swim, your reserves are low or depleted. It's important to replenish depleted glycogen stores immediately after a workout and to consume adequate protein to help repair muscle tissues.

After a workout or race, you have a limited window of opportunity to optimize the refueling process, which begins when you stop exercising and lasts for about two hours. Within 30 minutes of finishing your swim, eat a hearty snack that contains at least 0.5 gram of carbohydrate per pound of bodyweight, in addition to 20 to 25 grams of protein to help build and repair muscle tissue (three ounces of tuna or salmon, four ounces of skinned chicken or turkey breast or one cup of cottage cheese will do the trick).

Eating a meal within two hours of your race or swim is also crucial. It's easy for many swimmers to eat a good dinner after an evening workout, but for those who swim Masters in the morning, make an extra effort to consume a real meal. Long-term failure to adequately replenish glycogen stores can lead to tissue breakdown and fatigue.

And while you may do a great job of watching what you eat at home, what happens when you travel to a race? Are you tempted by fast-food and chain restaurants that serve high-fat, high-calorie crap? Don't blow your diet away from home. The days leading up to an event are critical for optimal performance. Pack food from home and stop at a local grocery store to stock up on fresh fruits and vegetables. Try to follow your normal diet as closely as possible.

TAKE-AWAY ASSIGNMENT – INTERNAL WARMTH AND NUTRITION

In conjunction with Lesson 1's Take-Away Assignment (exposing yourself to cold water), experiment with a variety of easily digestible foods or liquids that will enhance your internal warmth. Think of your body as a thermos. Wear a wetsuit, cap and goggles to keep the exterior warm and then fuel it up with something warm. Suggestion: try zapping a Clif Bar for 10-15 seconds in the microwave BUT for the luv of Pete, make sure you take it out of the foil wrapper first!

LESSON 3 – MENTAL PREPARATION

MISTAKE: Convince yourself, of 35,000 souls who successfully have swum Alcatraz you're going to be the one to get eaten by a shark, drown or otherwise die in your attempt.

LESSON: The single, absolute, most difficult part of swimming Alcatraz is all the negative mental stuff you beat yourself up with between now and the time you jump in the water! Once you jump in and start swimming, you're going to have the time of your life. (Fellow *Alcatraz Swimming Society* member Steve Hurwitz swears the most difficult part about swimming Alcatraz is finding parking downtown.)

In my first few months of swimming at Aquatic Park, I remember being perified (that's a lethal combination of being petrified and terrified at the same time) of what couldn't be seen but what had to lurking in the murky water just waiting to attack. This from a college graduate who intellectually knew since the South End Rowing Club was founded in 1873 not a single swimmer has ever seen a shark in the Bay much less been bitten by one.

Now I'm not going to lie to you. Yes, there are sharks throughout the Bay – five species to be exact. There's the Spiny Dogfish, a little 3-footer, who feeds on crabs, small octopus, fish and fish eggs.

Then there's the equally small Brown Smoothhound Shark, another 3-footer, who feeds on crabs, shrimp, worms and small fish (talk about bad karma, these poor guys are preyed upon by sea lions). Next we have the Soupfin Shark, prized by fisherman prior to the 1960's for their fins; these 5-footers are transients who only enter the Bay in the spring and summer for breeding and birthing. Fourth on the list is the attractive Leopard Shark which can reach up to six feet and who is a bottom feeder thrusting its face in the mud to capture shrimp, clams, crabs, worms, etc. And largest on the list is the Sevengill Cowshark which can reach 10 feet in length and weigh up to 350 pounds – these guys are masters of stealth and prey primarily on other sharks as well as seals.

If you'd like to see a Sevengill in action go to http://www.youtube.com/watch?v=dSmKfRKBphg or just type "Shirley the Sevengill Shark" in the YouTube search engine. This is Shirley, a nearly 10-foot 350 pound specimen who formerly was in residence at the Aquarium of the Bay in San Francisco. According to the March 12, 2009 notes accompanying the video – "Shirley is now swimming free in San Francisco Bay. We let her go right around Alcatraz Island, where we caught her initially."

Now before you throw up your arms, start screaming and start questioning your sanity for signing up to swim Alcatraz, here's yours truly swimming with a Sevengill Shark in the National Aquarium of New Zealand in December of 2009 (http://www.youtube.com/watch?v=riXzz4P4eok or just type "Shark Petting Zoo" in the YouTube search space). Like Shirley, this shark was a softie and let me pet her 5 or 6 times as she cruised through the aquarium.

For an informative and short article on sharks in the Bay, read Bay Nature's "Peering into Muddy Waters: The Sharks in San Francisco Bay," found at http://baynature.org/articles/apr-jun-2001/peering-into-muddy-waters.

Gary Giving a Massage to a 7-Foot Sevengill Shark
(at the New Zealand National Aquarium – Napier NZ)

The point I'm making is, yes, there are sharks in the Bay but they don't have the slightest interest in you. They're as apt to deviate from their normal food supply and snack on you as you are to forego your Whopper or Big Mac and go after the rats that live in the garbage bins behind these fine food dining establishments.

Think about it from another perspective: sharks are predators, creatures of opportunity. Put yourself in the shark's place – even the hungriest of sharks. Would you want to mess with a crowd of 800 to 1,800 strange, unfamiliar creatures who are beating the water? Would you want to be anywhere near those noisy machines zipping all over spewing out nasty gas and oil?

Face it! Not to be the one to spoil the important image you may have of yourself, but of the 35,000 people who have swum from Alcatraz and of the thousands from the Dolphin and South End Rowing Clubs who have been swimming in the Bay for over 130 years, you are NOT the one wearing the sign that says to the sharks: "Eat Me!" (Just to be on the safe side and to hedge my bets, I did give up eating shark meat after starting to swim in the Bay and in the ocean off Pacifica where there are Great Whites. It's something along the lines of "I won't eat you if you don't eat me." I also wear a special dolphin ring talisman, just to be on the safe side you understand. I hope I'm doing enough to keep my Mojo working.)

"But what about the Great White Sharks?" people often ask. "I thought the ocean right outside San Francisco is known as the Bloody Triangle because of the huge population of Great Whites." Well, the "men in the grey suits" (as we call them locally) are out there and for years people commonly believed they didn't come in the Bay. All the sediment from the 16 tributaries that drain into the Bay messed up their gills. However, more recently scientists discovered this may not be completely true. As part of a study between 2000 and 2008 conducted by Stanford, UC Davis, the Point Reyes Bird Observatory and the Pelagic Shark Research Foundation, acoustic tags were affixed to 179 Great Whites. Acoustic listening devices were placed at dozens of locations in the Bloody Triangle. Whenever a tagged shark came within 850 feet of the receiver, a code for that unique shark was recorded.

The study, released in November 2009, noted the listening devices detected five Great Whites by the Golden Gate Bridge in 2007 and 2008 though they don't know what the sharks did or how long they stayed (yikes - please put one of those monitoring devices at the opening to Aquatic Park).

Several more anecdotes to put it all in perspective. On the afternoon of June 20, 1996, surfers in the line-up at Linda Mar State Beach in Pacifica (about 15 miles south of San Francisco), spotted a 15-foot Great White Shark about 40 feet away from them. Within moments the water turned bright red as the shark nailed a seal and began thrashing it about. More recently, on July 15, 2010, a Great White jumped out of the water in full breach about 300 yards off the Linda Mar beach; and a month later, on August 30, 2010, a 20 foot Great White was seen devouring a sea lion just offshore. But these are classic good news, bad news stories. The bad news is, yes, there are sharks out there. The good news, and this is what you should remember, is they are not interested in us as a food source. They do recognize the difference between seals and surfers. If Great Whites were interested in us, they'd always be hanging around Linda Mar Beach since surfers are out from sunrise to sunset every single day of the year.

So what else can you worry about? Well, there are harbor seals and sea lions in the Bay. Both are two of the most curious animals you'll ever encounter. They're also very elusive. They'll frequently sneak up behind you to see what's going on and check you out. The ONLY way you'll ever even know they were behind you is when you get onshore and one of your fellow swimmers comments on the seal or sea lion that was right behind you.

Harbor seals have spotted coats and range in color from silver / grey to dark brown. They can get up to four or five feet and weigh over 200 pounds. They also have no external ears sticking out.

In the fall of 2003, I discovered the true meaning of "stark terror" (or was it "shark terror"). About 250-300 yards off the opening to Aquatic Park, an ominous black shape cruised back and forth right below me several times. It happened so fast and the water was so murky it was impossible to tell what it was. I could only think the worst. As you can imagine, sheer stark terror took over! I stopped swimming for a second and then realized I did not want to be a sitting duck so I swam like a man possessed. Right at that moment "it" buzzed under me again several times. At this point, I figured I was shark sushi and that "it" simply was deliberating as to what cut of meat "it" wanted first.

Lifting my head out of the water to see if I could attract the attention of the closest pilot, "it" jumped out of the water right in front of me. "It" turned out to be a very large, inquisitive and obviously playful seal. This guy was so full of playfulness and spunk that he actually leapt into the escort boat and startled the bejeebers out of the pilot.

Seals have never been known to bite any swimmers though there are numerous instances of playful pups bumping swimmers. Over the past several years, "Nibbles" (as we affectionately call her) visits Aquatic Park occasionally. Hapless swimmers, minding their own business, all of a sudden feel Nibbles bump them in the leg – a close encounter so unexpected most swimmers find they momentarily defy the law of gravity and fly five feet out of the water. Nearly everyone completely freaks and starts swimming faster than Michael Phelps which is exactly what Nibbles wants them to do – run so she can chase them and bump them some more. In the four times I've been bumped by Nibbles I've taken a different tack. After I get over the initial "What the Hell was that?" I immediately stop swimming and remain stationary (ask any mailman what's the one thing you should **never** do when confronted by a dog: run). Nibbles surfaces about three to four feet away and gives me this "what's wrong with you – don't you know the rules?" look. Then she submerges again while I agonize over whether she's going to nudge me again with her whiskers. Moments later she surfaces again, desperately wanting me to "run" away so she can play some more. Finally out of boredom, she gives me a "you're no fun" look and goes after someone more willing to freak out and flee.

California sea lions are much larger (and noisier and more stinky – take a walk down the west side of Pier 39 on Fisherman's Wharf –

you'll have a whole new concept of "stink"). They're typically brown in color, can reach seven feet (and more) and weigh up to 1,000 pounds. They do have external ears and a dog-like face. While there are normally hundreds of them in the Bay, they usually leave you alone unless you choose to insult them. A number of years ago, a group of South Enders was doing their daily sunriser swim and came across a rather large and curious male sea lion. Deciding to have some fun, one swimmer began barking at the sea lion. Having not taken the Rosetta Stone course in Sea Lionese I imagine he made some disparaging remark about the creature's mother because the sea lion snarled its lips, showed its teeth and came charging straight at the offensive swimmer. Terrified, the swimmer curled up into a ball, placed both hands over his privates and watched the sea lion (all 800 pounds) torpedo straight at him only to submerge seven to eight way-too-close feet away. The swimmer wasn't attacked but he did feel the draft of the sea lion speeding beneath him. Unless you can say "My, you're looking lovely this morning" in proficient Sea Lionese, just nod your good morning, keep your mouth shut and keep swimming. (However, if you're piloting a swim in a kayak or zodiac and it's your friends in the water then it's OK to bark all you want at them because you're not in any danger, just your friends.)

In the fall of 2006, a rogue sea lion in San Francisco bit at least 14 swimmers in Aquatic Park and chased numerous more out of the water. Biologists were baffled by the sea lion's behavior theorizing that he was perhaps protecting his harem or that he might have temporary brain damage from toxic algae (i.e. doing drugs). One of the old-time club members said that in his 70 years of swimming in Aquatic Park nothing like this had ever happened before. Well, he didn't have long to wait til the next episode. In the summer of 2009 another drug-induced attack came, a number of swimmers were bumped and one received a nasty bite on his thigh.

Just remember, these are very isolated and rare happenings. But you are swimming in their territory and encounters will occur every great once in a while. In a big race with hundreds of others around you, your chances of being bumped are miniscule .

Aquatic Roller Derby, Anyone?

So, is there anything else of which to be afraid? NO, but there are some things that can spook you if you're not prepared. First, there can be debris in the water, especially after a bad storm, so pay attention and keep an eye out – it's always a shock to hit something because your instant thought is "it's alive – I'm lunch!" Second, there are jellyfish in the Bay (usually found in the spring and summer). Relax, they DON'T sting but when you hit one, it's like touching a slimy piece of Jello. It's even more fun when you swim through a whole school of them. Again, relax, they've got just as much right to the water as you do and they find it equally repulsive to smacked by your naked hairy hand.

Getting a little more serious, the point I'm making is the more open water experience you get under your Speedo's, the more comfortable you'll feel in the water in all kinds of conditions (more on open water training in the next lesson). Where I used to be deathly afraid of swimming in the dark, one of my greatest winter pleasures is swimming in Aquatic Park early in the morning when it's still pitch black out. Watching the luminescence of the bubbles in the water and stopping to gaze at the lighted cityscape is a rare treat. Feeling totally comfortable and at ease in darkness didn't happen overnight. It happened over the course of time and many, many swims. (I still get a little nervous if I swim in Aquatic Cove before dawn when there's a full moon – I can't help but wonder what my body looks like silhouetted by the moon from ten feet underneath the water and whether 350-pound Shirley, the Sevengill Shark, is nearby.)

And no matter how many times I swim from Alcatraz I still get butterflies, which is normal. I simply remind myself of my own advice: the most difficult part of swimming from Alcatraz is all the mental stuff going on in my brain before I jump in the water. I know once I'm in the water I'm going to have a great time. As Tom Petty says: "the waiting is the hardest part."

TAKE-AWAY ASSIGNMENT – MENTAL ACCLIMATIZATION

Find an open body of water (cold, tepid or hot makes no difference) in which to swim safely where simply the unknown of what's in there makes you a little squirrely and edgy. An equally acceptable alternative is to swim in a familiar body of open water at night or before sunrise (if it can be done safely and with someone accompanying you for safety). Keep doing it until you've exorcised all your mental demons.

LESSON 4 – OPEN WATER TRAINING

MISTAKE: Decide you don't need to practice in the open water before your open water swim.

LESSON LEARNED: You wouldn't get ready for racing in a trail run by doing all your training on a treadmill or a track. Get out of the pool and train in open water!

Stroke Technique

Are you tired of grinding out grueling, lung-sucking pool work-outs month after month, exhausting yourself, yet never really getting faster? Did you ever wish there was some other way? Well, there is – by making sure you have good fundamental stroke technique. While it's best to have a competent coach videotape your stroke and give you feedback, you can improve your stroke technique using my "12 Tips for Aqua-Dynamic Excellence" to assess your current efficiency in the water.

1) Aquatic Wind Tunnel

All of us have tooled down the highway at some time in life with one hand out the window, feeling the force of the wind. Keep your hand flat and horizontal, pointed down the road, and the wind rushes right by. Lose that aerodynamic position and your hand is flung perpendicular by the power of the wind's pressure.

The same principle applies to swimming. Water is over 800 times denser than air so there's a lot to be said for minimizing your frontal surface area while swimming through water. Few swimmers devote enough time refining their stroke to reduce drag. Instead, most swim harder in the hopes of muscling their way to faster times. Focus on maintaining a body position that minimizes how much water you have to swim through. I always tell people to visualize swimming through the smallest tunnel possible so you're getting through the water easier. Just as downhill skiers maintain a good tuck position and just as we have aerobars on our bikes to reduce wind drag, envision yourself swimming through an *Aquatic Wind Tunnel* with your body as streamlined as possible.

2) Swim Long

In the 1800's a ship architect by the name of Froude came up with an interesting mathematical equation. Greatly simplified it says the fastest a sail boat can go is the square root of its length at the water line (e.g. a 36 foot ship can go 6 knots, a 25 foot ship can go 5 knots). The same applies to your body while swimming. Maximize your boat length by keeping your forward arm extended. I always tell myself to get one or two more inches out of my forward reach before starting my pullback – I reach and then glide for a quick second. I stay on my side longer and expose less of my body surface to water resistance.

3) Hip Power

Ever watch a golfer or baseball batter? Where does the power come from? Not from the arms but from the hips. The same is true in swimming. Your real power comes from your hips. In Australia, the Aborigines have spear slings called Atlatls that allow them to hurl the spears a further distance. Closer to home, many dog owners use dog ball throwers so they can throw Fido's ball further with greater ease. As it relates to swimming, visualize your hips (Atlatls / dog ball thrower) initiating the extension of your forward arm (spear / ball) into the water. When your forward arm extends, it's the snap of your same-side hip that should launch the extension. This helps get you on your side where there is less body surface exposed to the oncoming water. Think about it – a sail boat slices through the water quickly while a barge has to muscle its way through the water. Use your hips to launch your forward arm extension and get you on your side

4) Neutral Finger Position

Assess the position of your fingers as they enter the water. All five digits should enter together in a neutral position to maximize critical forward glide and extension. If your hand enters with your thumb first and your palm pointed outward you have to turn your hand underwater to initiate your pull which places undue pressure on your shoulder. The same thing applies if your hand enters with the little finger: you have to turn your hand underwater to start your pull. Focus on a neutral finger position as they enter the water.

5) Hand and Arm Entry

Assess your hand entry. Your hand should enter the water slightly in front of your head. Then your wrist, forearm, elbow and upper arm should all go through the same hole made by your hand. If you find yourself slapping the water with both your hand and your elbow at the same time, chances are you're not letting the downward snap of your hip drive your arm extension. You can make a game out of this by seeing how quietly and how few bubbles you make during your hand and arm entry – the less noise and fewer bubbles the more efficient your stroke.

6) Anchor and Pull

In Tip 2 I mentioned keeping the forward hand extended underwater just a little longer so you can glide and get another inch or two out of your stroke. This also allows you to anchor your hand securely in the water before pulling back. Pay attention to the water gliding over your finger tips and don't begin your pull back until you feel the flow of water over your finger tips diminishing. Make sure you maximize your pull leverage by using both your hand and your forearm. The best way to learn proper pull position is to practice fist drills. Close your hands into fists and swim several laps – it won't take long to learn where the best position is to grab more water. One-arm swimming drills do the same thing. Put your left arm out in front of you and then just swim with your right arm (then visa versa) – you quickly learn the best pullback arm position. Did you ever wonder why so many wetsuits have a different material on the forearm? It's designed to help you grab more water – learn to use your forearm.

7) Exit Hip / Hand Along Body

Assess the path and position of your recovery hand as it exits the water and extends forward. Practice dragging your fingertips slightly above the water's surface from your hip to your armpit, keeping your hand close to your body. Alternately, practice dragging your thumb up your body from your hip to your arm pit. Both these drills reinforce a high elbow and ensure proper hand position (below your elbow) for your next forward extension.

8) Front Quadrant Swimming

The term "front quadrant swimming" was coined by Terry Laughlin of Total Immersion and relates to "Tip 2 - Swimming Long." Your recovery hand and arm should be in an arc position over your ear before your other arm begins its pull back. This technique guarantees you always have one arm in the water forward of your head which helps keep your boat long. Don't forget to launch your forward arm extension with the snap of your hip. Ideally, you should snap, extend and glide on one side then snap, extend and glide on the other. This technique produces a different stroke rhythm than the typical arm windmill.

9) Flutter Kick from Hips

Do you churn up the water with your legs or kick from your

knees? If so, you're needlessly expending energy that you need later on the bike and run. Instead, flutter kick from your hips with minimal knee bend, using two or four kicks per stroke cycle (cycle being both a left arm stroke and a right arm stroke). The main purpose of kicking is to keep your hips and legs buoyed up in a horizontal body position. With a wetsuit, it's already doing this job for you and there's even less need to kick strenuously.

10) Neutral Head

Is your head position affecting your horizontal body alignment? If you look forward with your neck tilted slightly back then your neck is probably driving your hips and legs down which isn't optimal for buoyancy, speed or staying in the Aquatic Wind Tunnel. Keep your head in a neutral position between breaths and when not sighting and aim with the top of your head rather than with your forehead.

11) Alligator Eyes

When you sight do you lift your head up so much you throw your body off its horizontal axis and out of the Aquatic Wind Tunnel? To avoid this, practice alligator eyes: take a breath, glance forward slightly then put your head back in the water. Some swimmers might find it more natural to glance forward slightly before turning their head to breathe so try sighting both ways to see which feels more comfortable to you. The most important part of sighting is to keep only your eyes above the water like an alligator.

12) One-Eye Breathing

Do your mouth and nose barely come out of the water when you breathe? Ideally, when breathing, you should have one eye above and one eye below the water line. Use your body rotation to facilitate your breathing instead of turning your head and twisting your neck.

Summary

Next time you go to the pool, see how you stack up against "12 Tips to Aqua-Dynamic Excellence." You'll probably score well on some tips and need significant improvement on others. Focus on one skill at a time, preferably the one needing most attention. Science says it takes up to 15,000 repetitions to reprogram the body's automatic muscle memory so be patient. If you're swimming 30,000 yards a month, it will take you several weeks of concentration. By adopting the skills to become more aqua-dynamic you'll have a higher return on your training investment than simply swimming harder and stronger.

Train Like You Race

Would you feel 100% prepared for a trail run if all your training had been done on a treadmill or at the track? The answer should be obvious. How then can you expect just pool work to get you ready for an open water swim?

While there are similarities between swimming in a pool and open water, let's highlight the notable differences:

Pool / Practice	Open Water / Race Day
A lifeguard or coach nearby	An escort boat possibly 100 yards away
A black line on the bottom	No visible markings in the water
Muggy indoor air	Brisk cool morning
80-85 degree water	55-75 degree water
Swim suit	Wetsuit – chafing / tight in the chest
Flat water	Chop and / or waves
Excellent water visibility	Limited water visibility
A wall every 25 – 50 yards	500 -4,000 yards with no land

Overhead lights	Glaring sun, overcast or fog
Fresh water	Salt / brackish / aftertaste
2 – 6 swimmers per lane	50-200 swimmers mass start

The contrasts are striking! This explains why so many athletes who limit their swim training to the pool:

- Get nervous or panic being far from shore
- Have difficulty sighting
- Swim a crooked line
- Lose the nice form and rhythm they have in the pool
- Panic when choppy water or waves smack into them
- Hate the body contact of all those flailing arms and legs
- Feel anxious about the swim days before the race
- Can't wait to get through the swim in a triathlon so they can get on to the bike and run

Pool workouts are great for refining technique, building strength and developing endurance but you need to practice in open water to be confident and comfortable with whatever water conditions you encounter on race day. Confidence and composure are the basic building blocks of successful open water swimmers. They don't hyperventilate and gasp for air when they first jump in. They don't worry about being sushi on the shark buffet table. Waves crashing on top of them doesn't derail their mental concentration.

But how can you develop this same feeling of oneness with the water? It's really not difficult. If you've ever transitioned from road cycling to mountain biking, remember how you had to spend time in the saddle until you felt comfortable in the off road environment? It's the same with open water – with each outing you gain more confidence and composure. After a while you find yourself looking forward to these workouts – guaranteed. Some of you may not get to swim regularly in open water so seize every opportunity that presents itself. It's not realistic to do all your swimming in the pool and then expect an easy transition to open water.

Another reason for training in open water: a 1.5k open water swim can require up to 39% more strokes than its swimming pool equivalent! "What the Hey," you ask?

In a 25-yard pool, my stroke count is 18 strokes per length or 1,188 for 1.5k (18 strokes x 66 lengths). I recently swam in a 50-yard pool (yes yards not meters) and thought 36 strokes would take me from one end to the other. Imagine my surprise when I had to take 43 strokes. There was a marker at the 1/2 way point so I counted the number of strokes during the first 25 yards and during the second 25 yards. Sure enough, after the first 18 strokes (with a wall push-off) I reached the 1/2 point but it took me another 25 strokes to swim the second half with no wall push-off. The wall push-off is equivalent to 7 strokes! Extrapolating this to a 1.5k open water swim I'll take 1,650 strokes (25 no wall push-off strokes x 66 lengths). This is 39% more than my normal 1,188 strokes in a pool. This is huge!

Does this also affect my time? You bet! In a 25-yard pool, I swim 1.5k in 27:50 or 25.3 seconds per 25 yards. During my 50-yard pool session, instead of 50.6 seconds length (2 x 25.3), it took me 55.0 seconds: 25.3 seconds for the first 25 yards when I pushed off the wall and 29.7 seconds for the second half without the wall push-off. Extrapolating to open water, I'll swim 1.5k in 32:40 (29.7 seconds x 66 lengths) or 17% slower than in the pool.

Let's examine how your pool workouts can negatively affect your open water training and race preparedness.

First, and considering the examples above, your average 2,500 yard pool work-out probably is closer to 2,000 yards due to the sling shot effect of pushing off the wall; and your pool times don't reflect your slower open water speed. Second, since accurate sighting arguably is the least developed skill of many new open water swimmers, the resultant inability to swim a straight line can increase the distance up to 5%, especially if the course is not marked well. Third, throw in some current, chop and wind and your 1.5k race-day swim is now a formidable challenge which has been known to cause more than a few people to panic. Last, for many triathletes, your swim work-out likely is the first to fall by the wayside when struggling to balance family, work and training.

Bottom line on race day: you swim a *longer* distance than what you *undertrained* for in a time far *slower* than you expected.

What's an aspiring open water swimmer to do? The easy answer is to train in open water but this is not practical for most of you during the winter; and admittedly, coached pool workouts (such as US Masters Swimming) afford an opportunity to focus on speed work, drills and technique. The practical answer is increase the yardage in your workouts to compensate for those 7 strokes per length you don't take because of the wall push-off. If your current workout is 2,500 yards increase it to 3,000 yards or more. Make sure they're quality yards with emphasis on streamlining your body movement through the water.

Open Water Workout Suggestions

Most open water swimmers swim one straight long set but with a little creativity and imagination you can create and simulate a pool workout complete with a warm-up, drills, intervals and a cool-down.

Here are some open water training suggestions to give you the edge over your pool-only competitors.

Safety

First and foremost, swim with friends. You can also use them to help simulate race day conditions (see below). If you must swim alone, swim along the shore where you can easily stand up and wade out if problems arise. Avoid any location where boats may pose a threat.

Nutrition

Eat or drink what you normally do before a race. Make sure you're sufficiently hydrated as cramps are more likely to happen if you enter the water dehydrated and the consequences of cramping can be much more drastic in open water than in the pool.

Warm-up

Do a nice, leisurely warm-up but take note of any water conditions, currents, wind or waves that can affect your workout.

Intervals

Measure a set distance (very easy these days with a GPS and Google Earth), count your strokes or set your count-down timer for a 30- to 60-second sprint. During a race you may need to accelerate at the onset to get away from the pack, to move from one group of swimmers to another, to get back in the draft zone of the swimmer ahead if you lose it, to kick harder and get blood flowing to your legs as you near the finish or to sprint away from the swimmer who has been drafting off you the entire race. Regardless of how you measure the sprint, alternate it with a time period of moderate swimming three or four times longer than the sprint. Repeat as necessary. Your objective is to accelerate as necessary without wearing yourself out.

Main Set

Swim at a good clip (not quite race pace) for half to two-thirds the distance of your upcoming race. Use this time wisely and practice your sighting, drafting and buoy skills. Use "alligator eyes" while sighting.

Drafting is legal in open water swims and it can save you a 10 to 30 percent expenditure of energy. The best drafting position is 6-12 inches behind the feet of the swimmer ahead of you. Stay close enough to the swimmer so you can tuck into his or her slip stream but not so close you're constantly slapping their feet. (You can definitely feel when you're being sucked along behind a swimmer just as much as you can tell when you've lost the slip stream.) How closely depends on how much kick and bulk the swimmer ahead has (the bigger the kick and the bigger the bulk the greater the draft). An important thing to remember – make sure the person you're drafting off is swimming a straight line. You'll lose any drafting advantages if the swimmer you're following is zigzagging all over the place.

Practice your buoy turns. What may be a spread-out line of swimmers always reforms into a tight group at buoys. Round them without slowing down (have another swimmer simulate the buoy). If you don't like body contact, stay 10 or 15 feet off the buoy.

Cool down

Do a nice, leisurely cool-down and review what worked well for you and what you still need to improve.

Simulated Start and Finish

If your race includes a beach start, begin your open-water workout by lining up on the shore and running into the water until it's deep enough (usually knee depth) to start swimming BUT make sure you first know the bottom condition. Is it sandy, muddy, rocky? Are there sandbars further out? Dolphin diving two or three times as you enter the water is popular but if the water is deep enough to dive then it's deep enough to swim. Use dolphin diving only when waves are breaking over you. Dive through or under the waves rather than trying to jump over them or bracing yourself until they wash past you.

If you're training with friends, bunch up in a close group, run into the water and swim 100-200 yards in an equally tight group so you can feel less terrorized with flailing arms and legs all about. Hint: wear your goggles under your cap so if you get bumped or kicked, the goggles will get jarred loose but not knocked off your head.

To exit the water, it's quickest to swim until you can touch the bottom with your hand (usually as shallow as your mid-calf) then stand and run out of the water with a high knee step. I always laugh when I see people stop swimming in waist deep water and then lose 15-20 seconds as they wade out. It's so much faster to swim until you literally run out of water. Many people dolphin dive to exit the water but if it's deep enough to swim it's faster to continue swimming. If there are breaking waves, you may get a ride by body surfing but be aware of hidden obstacles.

Smart training in open water is the key difference between those who go into a race fully prepared and confident and those who feel stressed and anxious. Don't let the pool cheat you!

TAKE-AWAY ASSIGNMENT – OPEN WATER SWIMMING

Have your stroke video taped by a competent coach – it will be very obvious what needs improvement. With just two to five specific stroke technique improvements, you can swim quicker and easier.

LESSON 5 – ESSENTIAL OPEN WATER SKILLS

MISTAKE: Expect flat water and lane lines in San Francisco Bay.

LESSON LEARNED: While your pool focus is to repeat one perfect stroke after another and maintain a fluid rhythm, in the San Francisco Bay and other open water venues your focus often is to adjust your stroke to the variable and choppy water conditions.

If you think about it, open water swimming can require skills and techniques completely different from those used in a pool where lane lines flatten the water and currents or waves are not a factor. While open water can be relatively smooth, sooner or later you will encounter a swim where rough water or a strong current forces you to change your methods. Waves may push your body to the side – impeding your forward motion. Waves also may wash over your recovering arm and prevent a clean hand entry. Choppy water may be so unpredictable and turbulent your stroke timing and placement is thrown off and you find it impossible to get into any kind of rhythm. There may even be times when you have to resort to breast stroke.

To facilitate our discussion, let's differentiate between two common types of rough water: Waves and chop. Waves travel in one direction – head-on, from your back, from one-side or from an angle. You either swim up and over them or you swim through them. (Don't confuse waves with the large undulating upward and downward swell of the open ocean.) Chop is many small waves coming from no discernable direction. (Look in your washing machine the next time it's on wash cycle). Chop is frequently created by exceptionally windy conditions or unseen underwater obstacles, as with the submerged rocks at Alcatraz.

You must learn to compensate for rough water and overcome these disruptive conditions. First, for novice rough water swimmers, these conditions can be especially frightening and disconcerting. Stay relaxed, retain your composure and focus on your breathing. Remind yourself you cannot sink with a wetsuit on; you are simply going to get tossed around a little. Lifeguards and other water support personnel are looking out for you and can be there in a flash if you wave your arm over your head. If necessary, float on your back for a few moments.

Bilateral Breathing

Odds are good a wave or chop will slap you in the face. This may force you to forego a breath cycle, swallow water or even inhale some water through your nose (hope you don't have a staff meeting immediately afterwards). Again, do not panic, retain your composure and get a full breath on the next stroke. If waves come from your normal breathing side, the ability to breathe bilaterally, i.e. breathe to both sides, is a big bonus since you simply switch to the other side. You may need to exaggerate your body roll or head turn in order to catch a breath without swallowing water.

In San Francisco Bay the winds frequently whip in from the west with waves crashing into you on your right as you swim south back to shore. If you only breathe to your right, you're going to be breathing water the entire swim. Therefore, bilateral breathing is a huge skill to have in your arsenal. If you can breathe with ease to either side, the benefit is obvious. Unfortunately, there is no magic bullet for learning to breathe bilaterally. As I previously mentioned, it takes 15,000 repetitions to reprogram your body so a new movement feels natural. Believe it! I spent the entire winter of 1992 in a pool swimming all my lengths while breathing bilaterally. Learning to breathe to my left side was the most unnatural thing I've ever attempted to do. By the spring of 1993, I could do it without feeling awkward and today it feels so normal that even in the hardest blowing westerlies I still find myself wanting to breathe to both sides.

Invest the time; the pay-back is three-fold. Your neck muscles are more balanced. You improve your sighting since you now look in two directions. And, most importantly as we've discussed above, during rough water conditions, when the waves hit your face from one direction, simply breathe on the other.

Sighting

Sighting (i.e. looking to see where you're going) goes hand in hand with bilateral breathing skills. In 1988 before learning to breathe to both sides, I entered my first triathlon, the Ocean View Triathlon in Norfolk Virginia. Pre-race jitters evaporated five minutes into the swim as I found myself leading the pack. Talk about a rush! During the next several minutes I envisioned building up a sufficient lead on the swim to overcome my fatness and slow bike and run times to win my age group. I was so stoked! Another five minutes into the swim I figured since the course was a counter clockwise loop and the buoys were on my left it might be prudent to look left to see where I was heading. Can you imagine my dismay when the swim pack was following the buoys 100 yards to my left and I was heading straight out into Chesapeake Bay. I lost so much time getting back on course I finished the triathlon third from last overall.

In an Alcatraz swim, if you don't sight frequently you may find yourself so off course, being sucked out towards the Golden Gate Bridge by the currents (more about the currents in the next section), that race personnel pick you up out of the water and reposition you. Yes, in an Alcatraz swim, if the swim director thinks you are too far off course and will not make the finish line, you are scooped up out of the water and repositioned in a more favorable location. And in some Alcatraz events, if support kayakers have to redirect you three times, you are pulled from the water and your race is over.

Let's look at it from another perspective. The typical swim from Alcatraz is approximately 1.5 miles. Without well-honed sighting skills, you can easily add an extra 1/4 or 1/2 mile to your race (unless you actually want to spend an extra 10 or 15 minutes in the Bay).

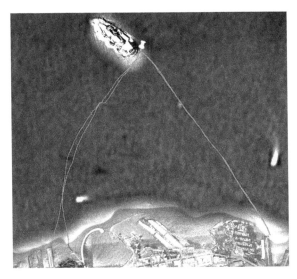

Sighting is Key

As you can see from this graphic comparison of two GPS-plotted routes, fellow *Alcatraz Swimming Society* member Allen Luong actually swam .3 of a mile longer than I did on our out-and-back swim. Good sighting skills can shave considerable time off your swim split without any extra effort or aerobic output on your part. By learning to swim a straight line from start to finish, you avoid zigzagging and adding unnecessary distance and time to your swim. In the instance of open water swimming, it's not always the fastest athlete who exits the water first but rather the one who can follow the best line.

So how do you know if you swim straight? At your next pool workout, close your eyes and without pushing off the wall swim until you bump into the lane line. Repeat the drill until you begin to notice a pattern. How many strokes do you take before you hit the lane line. If you hit the lane line every 5th or 6th stroke then sight every 5th or 6th stroke. Some swimmers can stroke 15 to 20 times before sighting while others need to sight more frequently. If the water is exceptionally rough you may need to sight even more frequently.

I breathe every 3rd stroke and sight every 12th stroke to take my bearings. This means I:

1) Breathe to my right, look forward to see where I'm going and stroke right,
2) Stroke left,
3) Stroke right,
4) Breathe to my left and stroke left,
5) Stroke right,
6) Stroke left,
7) Breathe to my right and stroke right,
8) Stroke left,
9) Stroke right,
10) Breathe left and stroke left,
11) Stroke right,
12) Stroke left,
And back to 1) Breathe right, look forward and stroke

In your closed eye swim drill, did you veer to the same side of the lane each time? If so, use this information to your advantage. If you veer to the right then position yourself to the left of the pack on race day to help you swim a straighter line. If you veer left then get on the right hand side of the pack.

Turbulent Water Considerations

Maintaining a stable body position is very important in rough water conditions. Picture a log and a rag doll in rough water – which has the most stability? To attain this stability, keep a long or log-like body position. This is best achieved by keeping a hand anchored throughout the entire stroke cycle. Keep your arm extended in front of you, hand firmly anchored in the water, until your other arm is about to enter the water – an almost open water "catch-up" stroke, if you will.

By keeping more than a normal amount of your body weight in front of your chest, you maintain a long-axis body position, which equates to good body-core stability. Good stability allows you to pull yourself through the choppy water much more effectively. Picture yourself piercing the waves rather than fighting them. The choppier the water, the more exaggerated your log-like body position and catch-up stroke.

Piercing the water also can necessitate altered stroke timing – either a shortened or prolonged arm recovery while you wait for the wave or chop to break. If you do not time your recovery right, you may grab air instead of water or find your recovering arm underwater as a wave passes over it. Do not be surprised to find yourself shortening or prolonging your timing on a stroke-to-stroke basis. Remember, rough water requires you to adapt your stroke to the conditions.

As I mentioned, waves coming from the side or an angle can push your body sideways. This can force your forward extended anchor hand out to the side or even downward. This is OK, because in this position your hand and arm now take on new roles. Your hand is not anchoring itself so your arm can pull your body forward (normal role). Instead, it is anchoring itself at your side to prevent you from being pushed sideways and to keep you in a forward line of travel (new role). This new role puts your arm in an awkward anatomical position and any attempt to pull yourself forward could damage your rotator cuff or sprain your shoulder. Let your hand and arm stabilize any sideways motion and then they can resume their more traditional job on the next stroke cycle.

A higher arm recovery can protect you from waves and chop. Forget the thumb-up-your-side recovery drill. Get your hand out of the water and high into the air quickly. Wait until the wave conditions are right and then quickly thrust it back into the water. You want to keep it away from the clutches of the waves.

Next, think about rock climbers. They want a good hold on a solid piece of rock before transferring their weight. Similarly, in rough water, you want to anchor your hand firmly in the water before you pull your body forward. However, rough water often is aerated due to the chop and waves. What you grab may not be solid water but a less supportive mixture of bubbles, foam and water. This makes it very important to practice catching more of the water with your forearm and ensuring that you push the water all the way back to your thigh without cutting your pull short. Most wetsuits have a different textured forearm to help you catch more water.

Currents and Body Position

In the Bay, the currents never cease and you may find yourself swimming into or against them. The key point to remember is the current will latch onto every single body protrusion it can find to thwart your forward progress. Increase your stroke rate and focus on swimming through that Aquatic Wind Tunnel. The current is flowing directly over your body and oncoming water wraps itself around even the slightest outcropping, increasing drag resistance and slowing you down. If you need to kick harder, do so, but keep your legs and feet in the Tunnel, limiting the depth of your kick to just below the surface.

If you find yourself swimming with the current, relax and enjoy the free ride. Lengthen your stroke, let the current do most of the work for you and marvel at how incredibly fast you are.

Read the Water

Last, learn to read the water and anticipate what it is about to do. With practice, you can spot the oncoming wave about to slap in you in the face during your next breath. You can see the oncoming wave that will force you to delay or accelerate the timing of your recovering armstroke. Anticipate the arrival of the next wave so you can sight precisely as you crest over the top of the wave and not while you are down in its trough, where your field of vision is obscured. The water has a lot to tell you if you only listen and pay attention.

TAKE-AWAY ASSIGNMENT – ESSENTIAL OPEN WATER SKILLS

Here's a take-away you can practice in the pool. While you're doing your warm-up or cool-down laps, practice your sighting both front and back. Pick an object on the wall at either end of the pool. Every several strokes (remember a 12-stroke cycle works for me) lift your head ever so slightly, see how quickly you can sight on the object and then put your head back down. If you practice sighting on your warm-up laps then practice, practice, practice and teach yourself to breathe bilaterally on your cool-down laps or vice versa. Breathing bilaterally and sighting are the most important skills you can develop in order to improve your open water swimming ability.

LESSON 6 – THE ACTUAL SWIM

MISTAKE: Believe swimming in San Francisco Bay is like swimming in a lake or ocean.

LESSON LEARNED: Swimming in San Francisco Bay is like swimming across a very fast flowing river.

Tapering

If you apply everything you've read up to this point, you're going to have a wonderful experience. However, I've got just a few more pointers for you.

Imagine, you've been working towards your Alcatraz swim or triathlon all year and the big event is just a couple of weeks away. All those long, hard grueling hours in the pool and those nervous open water outings are near an end. Don't make the most common mistake by continuing to work hard right up to race day. In the weeks immediately before an important race there's not much more you can do. However, there are several things you can do to sabotage your efforts and your readiness for race day. Many people overtrain in the weeks before their big event. They don't give themselves the proper amount of rest and recovery to be primed for a good swim on race day.

It's so very important to taper in the week to 10 days before your race. You need to decrease the number of yards you put in. If you average 3,500 to 4,000 per workout drop that in half. You can still include intense intervals in your taper workouts just reduce the number of intervals. This will allow your body plenty of time to rest and recover while still providing enough yardage to keep you sharp and fit. Don't forget to include an open-water swim once a week in your taper training.

Leading up to my 2009 12-mile solo Rottnest (Australia) swim, I swam 37,000 yards my last big week. The following week I dropped to 18,000 yards; the week after to 12,000 yards; and in the week leading up to Rottnest I scaled back to 8,000 yards. For 13 months I had swum so many yards each week I was dying to do more those last 3 taper weeks. But I didn't; and on the morning of the swim I felt fresh and gave it all I had. In fact, because of currents the 12 mile swim turned into a 14 mile swim. I was tired at the end but I could have kept going.

Check-out the Venue

For any swim, you also should familiarize yourself with the nature of the water conditions you'll be swimming in. For those of you reading this book, that's exactly what you're doing right now as you learn about the San Francisco Bay. But you need to do the same for other open water swims you plan to do as well. Investigate the conditions of your race's swim course by visiting the event website or by mapping out the area with the help of Google Earth. If your race is nearby, do an open-water swim there for a sense of temperature and environmental conditions. (Aquatic Park works exceptionally well for anyone getting ready for Alcatraz.) Based on the start time of your event, calculate whether you'll be facing sun glare. Identify fixed onshore landmarks in advance to help you navigate on race day. If your race includes a beach start or finish, practice running into the water and then running out again to a mock transition area or finish line.

If your race is out of town, you can get insider information on the event's swim course by talking to a representative from a local US Masters Swim club – at the least, he or she should be able to give you information on expected water conditions, temperature and other relevant details pertaining to the swim course. You can find an extensive listing of clubs on the US Masters Swimming website (www.usms.org).

The Swim

First, the disclaimer. There are NO guarantees Mother Ocean will cooperate with your plans for any open water swim, especially Alcatraz. During the last 15 years, I am aware of at least 5 commercial San Francisco Bay swims where an alternate swim had to be offered due to the dense fog that frequents the Bay (I've renamed the month of August "Fogust" because there is so much fog during the month). And based on my personal experience as a swimming participant in 794 scheduled Alcatraz swims since 1993, forty four (44) or 5.5% have been canceled due to adverse weather conditions (i.e. impenetrable fog, gale force winds, 4-foot chop or unpredictable currents caused by excessive rain run-off & snow melt). While you may feel disappointed if the swim is canceled or an alternate course plotted, the race director feels even more disappointed. Please bear in mind your safety is of paramount concern. Understand and accept that it's the responsibility of the race director to cancel the race if, in his judgment on race day for whatever reason[s], the conditions of the race do not offer sufficient safety and security of the athletes. As the saying goes, there are old pilots and bold pilots but there are no old, bold pilots. In other words, you'll live to swim another day. And for goodness sake, don't blame the race director – he has no control over the weather.

But today the sun is out, the weather is fine, the race is on, the ferry is taking you out to Alcatraz AND you are about to participate in one of the world's most exhilarating open water swim challenges.

All Alcatraz swims start with a jump from the ferry into the water. Depending on the ferry used, the jump height is between 4 and 6 feet. For a number of people, this is a terrifying experience though it shouldn't be. If you're one of these people then this is something you need to practice. Go to your local pool and start by jumping feet first off the low diving board (normally 3 feet). When this doesn't seem like such a frightening experience, head up to the high dive which is 10 feet. With just a little practice you'll soon overcome your fear.

The Jump

How you jump off the boat is important as well. Rather than jump off with your feet side by side, your toes pointed down and your arms at your side (which will just take you deeper under the surface), learn to do a lifeguard jump. Keep your legs splayed front and back, one arm out to your side and one hand shielding your goggles so they don't come loose or, even worse, come off.

Keep in mind there are anywhere from 500 to 1,800 other racers who have to jump. Jump in the water and IMMEDIATELY swim several strokes to get out of the way of the jump zone. The ferry exit is not the place to stop and ponder whether you're ready for the swim. You need to jump and get off quickly – typically, all swimmers are off the boat within 7 minutes. When you hit the water, don't fiddle with your goggles or readjust your cap or suit – get out of the way so the next group of people can jump.

If you've ever had insomnia and been up in the middle of the night, you may have seen one of those old World War II movies where the parachutists are jumping out of the back of the airplane – jump, jump, jump, jump, jump! It's the same with the jump off the ferry. Race directors normally find the biggest, meanest, baddest drill sergeants they can muster and make them exit door volunteers. They'll be yelling "jump, jump, jump" at the top of their voices – it's nothing personal - they just need to get everyone off in a timely manner.

It can be very chaotic and frightening so prepare yourself. Just know that when you reach the door you gotta jump and go quickly. One year people didn't get off the boat fast enough and the ferry drifted perilously close to Alcatraz. I was up in the wheel house with the captain and we both swear we could hear the vessel lightly kiss the rocks of Alcatraz.

As of this writing, there are numerous commercial Alcatraz events. Some take place during slack water and end up at Aquatic Park. All swimmers disembark and head for the in-water swim start normally formed by a line of kayakers. Once the last swimmer is off, the ferry horn signals the start of the event.

Others such as the *San Francisco Triathlon at Alcatraz*, the *Alcatraz Challenge Swim* and the *Alcatraz Challenge Aquathlon* take place as the current is ebbing (flowing out to the Golden Gate Bridge) and finish, depending on the event, at Marina Green, St. Francis Yacht Club or Crissy Field. The start of these events is different than the ones going into Aquatic Park. Because the current is moving west, it is impossible to keep up to 1,800 swimmers, 75 kayakers, 20 power boats and the ferry all stationary in one place until everyone has jumped in. Therefore, timing mats are placed at the ferry exit doors and your time begins once you step on the mat as you jump from the ferry (another important reason not to dawdle at the exit door).

Something else to consider, when you have this many people confined by kayaks and all heading for the same small finish area on shore a mile and a half away, you're going to experience the aquatic version of roller derby for the first 5-7 minutes. Prepare yourself and be patient. Before you know it the field spreads out and you have your own space.

On a personal note, while I mentally resign myself to share 12 square inches of water with 49 other swimmers during the first several minutes of the race, I have no tolerance for the person who keeps slapping my feet during the remainder of the swim. If you want to draft off me I don't mind; and I expect to get touched on the toes a couple or three times during the swim. What makes me a crazed person is when you keep slapping my feet throughout the entire swim. Here's what you can expect from me.

First, I've learned to urinate while swimming at race pace and the Cytomax does go through me pretty quickly. If I feel you hitting my feet more than a couple of times, I hope you're not swallowing too much water and you better hope I didn't eat asparagus for dinner last night. Second, if your rude behavior continues, I stop, draw my legs up to my chest and kick backwards as hard as I can. Maybe I'm a poor sport who should learn to ignore the idiot behind me but I make no apologies. There's plenty of room out there for both of us and I don't mind giving you a ride – I'm just not into constant body contact. In fact, I believe that not sending a physical message to these morons only serves to reinforce their inconsiderate behavior.

The River

Another important strategy for those of you doing the San Francisco *Triathlon at Alcatraz*, either of the *Alcatraz Challenge* swims or other events taking place on an ebb current is to understand the currents and use that knowledge to assist with your crossing.

Imagine, you're standing on the San Francisco shoreline looking out at Alcatraz in fast forward condensed time. The Bay is ebbing (emptying, flowing west to the Golden Gate Bridge) every 6 hours and flooding (filling up, flowing east towards Oakland) every 6 hours with water levels changing up to 8 feet. Four and a half million gallons of water per second through the narrow one-mile wide Golden Gate! This creates tremendous currents. In fact, they can exceed 6 knots (nearly 7 miles per hour for you landlubbers). To illustrate how quickly this is, the current record for swimming the 6 miles between the Bay Bridge and the Golden Gate Bridge with a strong ebbing current is an astounding 48 minutes! That's 8-minute miles. I don't even run that fast anymore! No wonder for years people believed (as many still do) that swimming from Alcatraz is impossible.

Who Pulled the Plug?
(The Water Dropped 8 Feet in 6 Hours)

This brings us to the most important principle about swimming Alcatraz. The San Francisco Bay is a fast flowing river that never stops. Repeat after me: the San Francisco Bay is a fast flowing river that never stops.

So how are people able to navigate these tricky currents? During the past 35 years, members of the 137 year old South End Rowing Club have learned to decipher the secrets of these incredible Bay currents. Let's look at the two routes used during commercial Alcatraz events.

Two Swim Routes

Marina Green / St. Francis / Crissy Field

If your swim leg of your event ends at Marina Green, St. Francis Yacht Club or Crissy Field, the race director times the swim to coincide with the ebb or outgoing current. The objective is to get across the channel as the current pushes you west. In essence you're forming a partnership with Mother Ocean. You swim south and she pushes you west. If you both do your jobs you float right into the swim finish. If you try to do her job and aim too far west, she gets angry and will kick your butt. I've learned this the hard way too many times.

There's also a very counter-intuitive aspect of who to follow on an ebb current Alcatraz swim. In most swims you simply follow the people up ahead of you. This can be a costly mistake here.

Think about it. Remember I mentioned it takes up to 7 minutes to get everyone off the ferry. If you're one of the last swimmers off the boat, the lead pack can already be a quarter or a third of a mile ahead of you and quite a bit to the west or right of you. Think about why they are west of you. They've been in the water longer, have swum further south (back to shore) and have been pushed further west by the "river" current. If you aim where they are, by the time you get there, the current will have pushed you even further west. Don't be lulled into following them. Stay your course. And pay attention to any corrections offered by the nearby kayakers: they know the Bay currents and some have been supporting Alcatraz events for years.

You Swim South (back to shore) & the Current Pulls You West

Aquatic Park

If your swim ends at Aquatic Park, the race director times the event around slack water, meaning when the current stops going one way and then reverses. Depending on the day, the current may either be flooding or ebbing when you begin but rest assured, the commonality is that halfway to two-thirds of the way across the current will shift and reverse itself.

With a flood start (filling up the bay), you first feel yourself pushed east (towards Oakland) and may try to over compensate by

90

aiming straight for the opening to Aquatic Park. This is a serious mistake since the current is going to reverse itself and head back to the Golden Gate Bridge as you near Aquatic Park. Stay to the left of the opening since it is much better to come in 100 yards east and float in on the current than it is to be 10 feet west swimming into a current so powerful you cannot make any headway.

With an ebb start (emptying the Bay), you feel yourself being pushed slightly west towards the Golden Gate Bridge. Again, the current reverses mid-way through the swim and you are pushed east, hopefully to the opening.

Suffice it to say, with an Aquatic Park finish, you've got an opening space of approximately 150 feet to aim for from a mile out in a rapidly moving current – it's like trying to thread a needle. If you don't or can't keep an eye on the opening you won't be positioning yourself advantageously. I've gotten my sighting down to such a degree I can tell from a half mile away the degree of adjustment I need to make. Using a method I call "triangulation" I pick the three masts of the Balclutha as my "benchmark" and then I pick another landmark on shore such as the twin Fontana Towers as my "directional reference." The objective is to keep the two landmarks and me lined up in a straight line. If see the Fontana Towers moving to the right or west of my benchmark, the Balclutha, then I know I'm drifting to the right or west as well. I correct by aiming east or to my left to bring all three of us back in a line.

Using the Balclutha and Fontana Towers to Stay on Course for a Swim into Aquatic Park

I also sight during the first part of the swim because I want to know right away if the current is stronger or weaker than predicted. I always joke that during the first half of an Alcatraz swim the best way to know where you're going is to know where you've just been. I use Alcatraz as my "benchmark" and Angel Island as my "directional reference." If I see Angel Island being swallowed up behind Alcatraz I know the current is pushing me west – if I start seeing more and more of Angel Island I know I'm being pushed east. The reason I do this initial triangulation is to swim a smart line. If the race director tells me to sight on the Fontana Towers I could be pushed to the Golden Gate Bridge, still sighting on the Fontana Towers and not know I was getting off course. So I regularly stroke and roll over on my back, locate Alcatraz and Angel Island, calculate how much I've drifted, then stroke and roll back onto my stomach. Better to adjust every couple of minutes by looking back than to get across the channel and realize the current has carried me way off course. And this kind of in-water navigation can help a slow swimmer have a quicker swim than a faster swimmer who doesn't pay attention.

To me the allure of Alcatraz is that it's a thinking swim – you constantly have to monitor where you are and what the currents are doing and make minute by minute adjustments.

Missed Finish

The bad news is each year many rookie swimmers or those who think they are more powerful than Mother Ocean or those who think the race directors exaggerate the power of the currents make the mistake of aiming too directly at the finish. They either overshoot the finish or they miss the opening to Aquatic Cove.

The good news is there are ways to salvage such mistakes. If you are participating in the swims taking you west towards the Golden Gate Bridge on the ebb current and you overshoot the finish, *don't waste precious time and strength* trying to swim back up against the current. You're only going to swim in place and not go anywhere. Instead, swim directly into the beach then run back and into the swim chute. It's much easier to run 100 yards back to the swim finish than battle your way against the frequently strong currents. **Very important:** *Make sure you go through the swim finish chute and over the timing mat or the race director will think you're still in the water; and the Coast Guard will be out in the Bay for hours looking for your body!*

For swims back into Aquatic Park, here are your fall backs. If you find yourself west of the opening fighting the ebb or outgoing tide, swim underneath the Muni Pier and back to the opening staying between the pilings and the concrete base of the Pier. These support pilings greatly reduce the current making it possible to swim back to the opening. The difference is so great a swimmer on the outside of the Pier may be swimming in place (or even losing ground) while the swimmer underneath the Pier is making progress.

If you find yourself east of the opening fighting a flood or incoming tide, stick as close to the breakwater as possible (the struts supporting the breakwater reduce the force of the current) or easier yet, signal to support craft to be picked up and repositioned.

Hopefully, you won't need these alternate escape routes but it's good to know they exist. In fact I wish I had known this on my very first Alcatraz swim. I was 200 yards away from the opening to Aquatic Park and aimed straight at it. Imagine my surprise as the "river" swept me right past the opening. There I was on the west side the opening swimming in place along Muni Pier but going absolutely nowhere. A kayaker came by and told me (and several) others to swim to the concrete abutment under the pier, climb on and wait for a power boat to come pick us up. We waited and waited and waited – no power boat. Finally, we realized the only way we were going to make it into Aquatic Park was to scramble over the hundreds of barnacles on the abutment and jump off on the other side. The cuts and abrasions lasted for weeks but at least we made it back into Aquatic Park.

Prominent Landmarks & Proper Sighting

Knowing how the currents in the Bay work is only part of the recipe for a successful Alcatraz swim. The other part is to know the prominent landmarks.

Depending on race day currents, the race director may have you sight on any number of onshore objects. It's important to recognize these and use them to guide you home since there are no buoys in the water to follow.

Furthest east is the *Jeremiah O'Brien*, a gray naval ship and one of the most commonly used landmarks for the first half of the swim. Next and close to one another are the *Eureka*, an old white paddle wheel steam ship, and the *Balclutha*, a red 3-masted schooner. Perhaps the most noticeable and frequently referenced land mark is the twin tower apartment building known as the *Fontana Towers*. Directly below is the very visible and very white *Maritime Museum*.

West of Aquatic Park is the squat square white *Pump House* at the foot of Van Ness Street (immediately to the west of Muni Pier). Immediately west of the *Pump House* is *Fort Mason:* 3 yellow & red buildings on wharves jutting out over the water. And for those of you swimming an ebb swim, the bronze doom of the *Palace of Fine Arts* and the bright orange roof of the *St. Francis Yacht Club* are two prominent landmarks. If the gods are smiling down on you race day, the sun will be out allowing you to sight on the goddess of all landmarks: the 977 foot orange and white *Sutro Communications Tower*. This is the perfect land mark to use for the ebb swims (the swims where the current takes you west towards the Golden Gate Bridge).

All of these landmarks are normally visible even with San Francisco's persistent fog. The only exception is the Sutro Communication Tower which likes to play hide and seek with the clouds and fog.

Jeremiah O'Brien – Far Left; Eureka (white boat) – Far Right

From Left to Right: Eureka (white boat), 3-Masted Balclutha and the Fontana Towers

From Left to Right: Opening to Aquatic Park, the Muni Pier, Sutro Tower, Pump House (square white building) and Ft. Mason

Palace of Fine Arts Dome – Far Left; St. Francis Yacht Club – Far Right

Putting It All Together:
(Can you spot the Jeremiah O'Brien, the Eureka, the Balclutha, the opening to Aquatic Park, the Muni Pier, the Fontana Towers and the Pump House?)

Swim Finish

As you finally approach the swim finish, what's the best way to exit the water? I've read in a number of articles that the "dolphin exit" is best (as you get close to shore push off the bottom into a forward dive, continuing with subsequent push offs until you can high-step it out of the water). I've found it much quicker to continue swimming until there is no more swimmable water – usually as shallow as mid-calf. (Rarely are waves at the swim finish more than one foot.) Then I stand and sprint up the beach. Whatever you do, don't stop in waist deep water and loose precious seconds muscling your way through the water to the beach! Last, remember your time isn't taken at water's edge. With today's timing chips, there's normally a timing mat somewhere up the beach – hustle until you cross over it.

TAKE AWAY ASSIGNMENT – THE ACTUAL SWIM

This drill will help get you past the panic you may experience in the first few chaotic minutes of swimming in a mass of flailing arms and legs. It works best with two friends but one will suffice AND, yes, this is another one you can do in the pool but trust me that it's more fun in open water.

Decide who's going to be the victim and who gets to have fun. The "victim" starts swimming normally while one friend swims right next to you – the goal is to see how close s/he can get to you including swimming right up on top of you if possible. Your other friend should be right behind you and his / her goal is to slap your feet and then to see if s/he can swim right up on top of your legs. Change places, have fun and don't worry about the people gawking in the next lane!

LAST THOUGHT

So there you have it. Over 1,000 miles swimming to and from Alcatraz. I've learned a lot – the HARD way. I encourage you to take my experiences and advice and try it out for yourself. Keep what works and toss the rest. And, if by any chance you learn something I still haven't, feel free to contact me at SFBaySwimmer@sbcglobal.net.

The addiction of Alcatraz is it's a thinking swim that's never the same twice – EVER! Best of luck and enjoy your experience. You will never fly in or out of San Francisco again without wanting to sit by the window and pick out Alcatraz and the route you swam. It amazes me still!

PART THREE:

Take My Job, Please!
What an Alcatraz swim is like, from the Perspective of
a Swim Director
Joe Oakes

"All of us are glad to get off. It's good for me and everybody. Alcatraz was never no good for nobody."

Frank Weatherford – the last prisoner to leave Alcatraz,
March 21, 1963

I have been directing swims in San Francisco Bay for 30 years, and have guided and directed about 30,000 swimmers from Alcatraz in that time. I want to put you in my shoes for a bit. Ready? Here goes:

Out of the blue you have been appointed Swim Director for one of the Alcatraz events, a totally new experience for you. (Run the other way *fast* if you value your sanity.) Your job is to move 1,000 swimmers, with an in-water start, from a point just south of Alcatraz to the beach at Crissy Field, a distance of about two miles. The expert (i.e. you) has selected the right tides and currents and has hired a ferry to transport the swimmers out to Alcatraz. Your job is to make sure that every one of them makes it safely from the point where they jump from the ferry into San Francisco Bay at Alcatraz, all the way to the beach at the swim finish.

WHAT GOES INTO PUTTING ON AN ALCATRAZ SWIM

Whoa! Wait a minute, Mister Swim Director. You don't just go out there and dump a bunch of people into the water at Alcatraz and yell 'swim'. There is a lot more to it than that, and the goings-on (otherwise known as work) will take months. Some decisions will have to be made a year or more in advance. Think of your project as a San Francisco version of the D-Day Invasion in World War II. There are three stages: Planning, team building and logistics.

Planning

Let's start with dealing with selecting the date and time of the swim. Every Alcatraz swim is controlled by the tides and currents, which in turn are a function of the phases of the moon, and to a lesser extent, the sun. There are usually two high tides and two lows a day, causing the water to pour in from the Pacific twice daily (*flooding* currents) and to dump back out of the Bay twice daily (*ebbing* currents), stopping briefly to reverse gears in between the ebbs and the floods (*slack* tide). If you want a lot of swimmers to show up at your event, you will have to put on your swim on a weekend morning. What you need to do in your planning is to pore through the tide tables and find a Saturday or Sunday morning when the phase of the current is just right to help your swimmers get from Alcatraz to where you want them to go. It is not easy, and it will probably occur only a few weekends per season.

Permits

San Francisco Bay is under the jurisdiction of the United States Coast Guard. If you want to put on an event in the Bay you will need their permission, and it must be requested long in advance. The Marine Event Coordinator will want to know everything about your swim, so you had best be prepared with a detailed swim plan. In addition to the Coast Guard you will have to work with the San Francisco Police Department, specifically with the Marine Division. That part of the Bay adjacent to San Francisco is within their jurisdiction, and that is where your swim will take place. Your swimmers will have to come out of the water someplace, and it will probably be within the shore area controlled by either the Golden Gate National Recreation Area (they have several sub-jurisdictions) or San Francisco Parks, each requiring permits, again far in advance. If the Golden Gate Bridge is involved, that may mean another permit requirement from yet another government entity. (One of your problems here will be that even though you may *apply* for your various permits very early, you will probably not get a response for several months, if at all. You may have to shell out money up front for fees, and show proof of insurance. It's a crap shoot.)

Getting to Alcatraz - the Ferry

Okay, you have all of your permits. How are you going to get the swimmers out to Alcatraz on race day? If you said the word 'ferry,' you are correct. So go out and find a ferry that will be available on the morning when you need it, willing and big enough to legally carry 1,000 swimmers out to Alcatraz. There are not very many of them. It is going to cost you big bucks, and they are not always available, so you had best do your search and book really early.

Advertising

How will you get the word out? Advertising? Where, how far in advance, and how much to budget for it? Who will design the copy?

Team Building

Directing 1,000 swimmers from Alcatraz is a big deal. You will need a lot of help, and your team had better know what they are doing. It is a very dangerous situation, and you will have to build a large and competent team for the task. They will have to be given very specific assignments and be prepped on just what they are expected to do under normal circumstances and what to do when the unexpected happens, *and the unexpected will definitely happen.*

My approach is to use an envelope of kayaks as the first line of defense for the swimmers. Backing them will be several power boats, a communications team and a medical team. There is a team coordinator for each team, and they are all kept in constant contact with each other on the water by radio. We have worked with the same cadre for several years, with little turnover. Your team coordinators will have to be on board at least several months in advance and will have to develop good rapport with their teams. We have developed our Alcatraz Swim Safety Team over many years. As of this writing our Alcatraz Safety Team leaders are Andy Guiliano (power boats); Bob Stender and Marc Paulsen (kayaks); Cissy Chase (medical); Barry Bettman (communications); Sue Free, George Rehmet, Danny Needham, Gary Emich and me, Joe Oakes.

If they are available, it is wise to make use of the services of Coast Guard and San Francisco Police units into the team. They are professional and well worth having on your team.

Logistics

Sponsors: What will they provide and how do you entice them? Insurance: where to get it, what is covered and how much is required? (If somebody gets hurt you can expect a lawsuit.) Sanctions: does the swim need to be sanctioned by USA Triathlon or US Masters Swimming? Porta-potties: how many, when and where? (One year they were delivered a mile from where they were needed.) Food for swimmers and volunteers; Water and energy drinks; On-shore volunteers for the dozens of jobs there; (They all need to be recruited and trained. How to do that effectively when you may never even see them until 0430 race day.); Timing system? Chips? How do you register swimmers? Will there be race day registration? Awards? What, how many? Will you give them something nice or just another cotton tee shirt to go into the drawer? Et cetera.

As I said, you would be better off to run the other way when offered the job of swim director.

Okay, the months of planning and preparation are behind you. It is race day and it is time for the swim. Here is your timeline. Note that it will vary from event to event, depending on conditions:

Zero Minus 90 Minutes

The Alcatraz Safety Crew has assembled in various locations: the kayak paddlers are on the launch beach at Aquatic Park, receiving route, current and safety instructions; The power boats are headed for the rendezvous point, coming from various marinas; the medical team is ready to board its boat; the communications ham operators are being briefed.

Zero Minus 60 Minutes

By this time all Alcatraz Safety Crew personnel are headed towards Alcatraz Island.

Zero Minus 30 Minutes

You are informed by radio that the ferry is loaded with 1,000 swimmers and is en route to Alcatraz.

Zero Minus 10 Minutes

The swimmer-filled ferry arrives at the exact point where the swimmers will start jumping into the water. You check on the various elements of your armada, and when you are satisfied that all of your swim Alcatraz Swim Safety Crew escorts are in place, you give the go-ahead to your contact on the bridge of the ferry via ham radio, with backup by cell phone and a previously agreed upon marine radio channel.

Time Zero

The ferry captain sounds his horn and the swimmers start entering the water. The first swimmers, often a group of professionals, leap several feet from the boat and immediately start swimming, then more and more and more jump through the boat's narrow doors, until all 1,000 are in the water. That process will take several minutes. By the time the last swimmer has left the boat, the leading swimmers might be a third of the way across the Bay.

The fastest swimmers move at about twice the speed as the slowest swimmers, so by the time the first swimmer reaches the beach the last ones will be less than half way across. That means that the pack will be spread out over a mile. Because some will swim further to the right and others to the left, the pack might be a quarter of a mile wide. The safety of every one of them is your responsibility.

The most dangerous time is at the very start. It is then that your Alcatraz Swim Safety Crew must be most alert. Before jumping six feet down from the ferry into the cold Bay, some competitors may be stressed out and choose to withdraw. It happens. They will be politely asked to move back from the door so others can enter the water. Because there are so many jumping from the ferry, it is imperative that those already in the water quickly get out of the way of the next swimmers leaping from the ferry in order to avoid being crowned by the next swimmer to jump. Entering cold water suddenly can be a shock, so it is not unusual for a swimmer to become temporarily disoriented. It is also the time when goggles can be lost. Swimmers will be excited and crowded closely together at this time of confusion.

Be alert for problems, Swim Director!

Time Zero + 10 Minutes

Because of the turbulence caused by the ebbing current ramming into Alcatraz Island (and the mountain of underwater debris that was dumped there years ago) there is always rough water in the first part of the swim, and it might take ten minutes for a swimmer to reach relatively smooth water. Swimmers just have to fight their way through that rough patch. After leaving the ferry they will aim towards specific landmarks on the shore, possibly a tower, a pier or a building, all of them over a mile away, sometimes not visible, enshrouded in fog. Slower and faster swimmers have been instructed as to the appropriate courses and sightings, but they have also been told that it is imperative that they follow the instructions of the paddlers who will be accompanying them, monitoring both the swimmers and the changing conditions. Some swimmers will pay attention, and others will be know-it-alls and create their own courses. The 'creative' ones just might have to be hauled from the water sooner (disqualified for course violations) or later (because they had to be rescued).

The fastest swimmers are required to follow the Lead Boat, which sets the course. The rest of the pack follows them, guided by one phalanx of kayaks to the left and another to the right. The swim pack will be shaped like a large 'V' following the Lead Boat.

Time Zero + 30 minutes

When that first swimmer reaches the beach, usually in about a half hour, the slowest ones will not yet have reached the half way point. A few of them do not belong there: they may lack the ability for this arduous swim. Others will start to feel the effects of being in cold water too long, especially if they (a small number) are swimming without wetsuits. Fatigue will be setting in. They have been told that if they need help they should signal a nearby kayak, who will summon power craft to assist the swimmer.

Now is a critical time for the Alcatraz Swim Safety Crew, and they are very alert to what is going on in the water. It is not unusual for five to ten percent of the swimmers to have to be helped from the water for one of several reasons. The most common reason is that because of their location in the currents (too far east, west or north) it has become impossible to reach the finish area. The second reason has to do with the condition of the swimmer, who either asks for help or it becomes clear to the experienced Alcatraz Swim Safety Crew escort that the swimmer needs assistance. Those swimmers may be boated to the beach or taken to a better location and be permitted to swim the rest of the way. The third reason for pulling swimmers might have to do with an unexpected condition arising, such as a sudden storm or an oil tanker unaware of the swim event.

Time Zero + 60 Minutes

All but a handful of swimmers have finished and the few remaining will have the individual attention of the Alcatraz Swim Safety Crew, good people, who, in addition to being there for safety reasons, are emotionally invested in helping these swimmers to succeed. In a few more minutes it will all be over, the last swimmer kissing the beach. The Safety Crew remains on site until word is reached from the Timing Crew that every swimmer has been accounted for. Now they too can beach their boats and get something to eat. And you can breathe knowing that your team has done a great job.

SWIMMER QUALIFICATIONS: AN ADMONITION

I will make this brief and to the point: A swim from Alcatraz is very serious business. It is never to be taken lightly. Over the years our Alcatraz Safety Crew has rescued over 1,000 swimmers, many of whom should not have been there in the first place. In order to succeed you must be a strong swimmer, experienced in long, cold swims in moving water. If that description does not fit you, I strongly suggest that you gain the experience necessary before attempting an Alcatraz swim.

The following are the minimum criteria you should use to judge whether you are qualified to swim from Alcatraz.

Distance

The distance swum in an Alcatraz swim is equivalent to 1.5 miles. Because of the currents, it can either shorter or longer. You should have the demonstrated ability to swim 1.75 in open water in a time of 75 minutes. This provides a margin of safety for those times when Mother Ocean decides to keep swimmers in longer than anticipated.

Rough Water

The water on this course is rarely flat. Normal chop is in the range of 6 – 12 inches, but can be larger. You should have the demonstrated ability to swim the full distance in choppy water or wave action.

Cold Water

Normal temperature range for this swim is 55-59 F. You should have the demonstrated ability to withstand exposure to cold water for 75 minutes wearing a wetsuit.

Wetsuits

Wetsuits are highly recommended for the Alcatraz swim. Swimmers opting to swim without a wetsuit should have demonstrated the ability to withstand exposure to cold water (55-59F) for 90 minutes.

Self-Policing

In the interest of your safety and well-being, you are expected to honestly judge your ability to meet the above criteria. If you do not meet these criteria, you should not participate in an Alcatraz swim .

PART FOUR:

The Protocols of the Elders of Alcatraz

Joe Oakes

"Failure to prepare is preparation for failure."

John Wooden

What is contained in this section is a very generous gift from the authors. It is a compendium of the protocols that we have developed for each of the Alcatraz Swim Safety Team disciplines. These have taken us many years to hone, and they are living documents, ready to be sharpened again as we continue to learn more. After every swim we ask for comments on how we might improve the way we put on our swims. It is our aim to strive for the unattainable goal of perfection.

You may feel free to use these protocols with our blessings, bearing in mind that they are merely pieces of paper, and that once you take them as your own, you are completely responsible for how you use them. Good luck!

If you are crazy enough to want our job, take it with our blessings.

SWIM START PROTOCOL

Over the years we have developed a rather straightforward swim start procedure that we feel affords maximum safety to both the swimmers and the support people. It is as follows:

Disclaimer: Canceling the Swim or Moving the Start

Swimming events in San Francisco Bay often are accompanied by unusual situations. No two swims are ever the same, and it is entirely possible that on a given day the forces of nature or man may make it impossible to do the swim as planned (as Gary noted previously, over 5% of his planned Alcatraz swims were canceled). In the event that conditions on the water indicate that the swimmers will encounter *unusually difficult or dangerous conditions*, the following procedure will be in effect:

Both the **Race Director**, who may be on the ferry, and the S**wim Director**, who must be on the Command Boat, are authorized to *either cancel the swim or move the location of start of the swim* to an agreed upon safer location. Such action by either party must be communicated immediately to the other party and to all concerned parties.

The Race Director and the Swim Director are to be in communication with each other by ham radio, marine radio and cellular telephone.

Conditions that might require these changes include dense fog, heavy wind, excessive chop, or traffic. Any of these may be sufficient for either a change of start location or a cancellation of the swim.

Assemblage

All safety personnel are to be on site prior to the arrival of the ferry. Because of the complexity of bringing people and water craft from various locations throughout the Bay to gather at the starting place, it is not always possible to all be there *exactly* on time, but we are never far off. (We typically have people arriving from Aquatic Park, the Saint Francis Yacht Club, Pier 39 and several marinas in the east bay, Marin and the peninsula. They sometimes come out through fog or rough seas.)

When the ferry arrives at the starting position, the Swim Director is in communication with the following personnel on board the ferry: Assistant Swim Director; Ham Operator; Race Director. Our channels of communication include ham radio; marine radio; and cell phone.

When the Swim Director decides that the team is in place and it is safe for swimmers to enter the water, he gives that information to his contacts on board the ferry via ham radio.

After it has been determined that all is in place for a safe swim *then, and only then*, is the signal given to start the race.

KAYAK PROTOCOL

The swimmer's first line of defense is the squadron of kayaks that escorts them to the swim finish. Kayak escorts are vital to this event.

Qualifications of Kayak Paddlers
- Paddlers must be experienced in open-water kayaking, including rough water
- Paddlers must be properly clothed for the bad weather that is often encountered at Alcatraz
- Paddlers must be 18 years old or older

Role of the Kayak Coordinator
- Recruits kayak paddlers, including determination of suitability of paddlers
- Issues a pre-race email outline of procedures for paddlers
- Gives an orientation to paddlers on the beach on race day
- Monitors and supervises the distribution of paddlers on the water during the race
- Sees to the compensation of paddlers: expense money, tee shirts, energy bars, after-race snacks
- Thanks the paddlers and seeks input from them for improvements

Orientation of Paddlers on the Beach
- Safety procedures
- Stress the importance of the job
- The predicted tidal conditions
- The swim route for that day
- How to handle emergencies
- Distribution of kayaks at the beginning of the swim and as it proceeds
- When paddlers may leave the swim

Organization on the Water

The Kayak Coordinator shall assign paddlers to 'pods' covering each physical segment of the swim route, i.e., sweepers, left flank, right flank, according to the needs of the day. During the race the kayak coordinator will constantly monitor the distribution of the kayaks and reassign them according to the needs of the race.

After the Swim

When all swimmers are safely ashore, the paddlers are invited to gather on the beach for refreshments. At that time the Swim Director should find time to thank them for their work and ask for their comments on how to improve water safety.

POWER BOAT PROTOCOL

Power Boats are used in Alcatraz swims for the following purposes:

• To escort the swimmers to the beach.

• To be alert to incoming boat traffic and if necessary, to intercept it.

• To be alert to kayaks calling for swimmer assistance.

• To bring swimmers from the water when in need of assistance.

• To transfer volunteers from shore to/from watercraft.

• To transfer swimmers from the water to the beach.

• To always see to the safety of the swimmers, their prime concern.

Description of the Fleet

Command Boat - The Swim Director uses this boat to monitor and control all aspects of the swim race on the water, including the start. He maintains contact with all other Power Boats via a communications system, described below. Personnel on board are the Swim Director, the Ham Operator Coordinator, the pilot and possibly a fourth person.

Lead Boat - The Lead Boat sets the course in front of the fastest swimmers. The course taken by the Lead Boat takes into account the fact that slower swimmers will react differently to the currents. Personnel on board are the Course Plotter, the pilot, a ham operator and an observer. The Lead Boat shall be easily identifiable by a large, brightly colored banner facing the swimmers.

Left (East) Flank Boat - The Left Flank Boat takes a position to the left of the main pack of swimmers, about halfway between the front and rear swimmers. It will display a large banner on its left side, indicating that there are swimmers in the water. This boat constantly scans the left of the pack for incoming boat traffic, immediately reporting traffic to the Swim Director and the San Francisco Police Department (SFPD). In an extreme situation, this boat will go to the incoming vessel to warn it of swimmers in the water. Personnel on board are the pilot, a ham operator and an observer.

Right (West) Flank Boat - This boat performs the same function as the Left Flank, but on the opposite side of the pack of swimmers. Same personnel as east flanker. Banner on right.

Sweepers - Sweeper vessels (there may be several) remain to the rear of the swim, spreading out evenly around the rear half of the pack of swimmers. This is where there is most likelihood of swimmers needing help. Sweepers are constantly watching for slower and/or troubled swimmers, and are prepared to remove swimmers from the water as required. They constantly observe the kayak paddlers in their vicinity for raised paddles, a signal that a swimmer needs assistance, and go to the aid of that swimmer. Personnel on board include the pilot and at least one observer. There may or may not be a ham operator.

Kayak Boat - The Kayak Boat serves the purpose of seeing to the needs and distribution of the kayak escorts around the perimeter of the swim pack. It must constantly be on the move adjusting the spread of kayaks, which sometimes have a tendency to gather together. See 'Kayak Protocol.' Personnel include the pilot, the Kayak Coordinator, a ham operator and maybe an observer.

Medical Boat - The Medical Boat remains to the rear of the pack with the Sweepers until called to aid swimmers elsewhere. Personnel include a pilot, a medical professional, a lifeguard, a ham operator, and possibly an assistant. See Medical Protocol.

Additional Boats - Shall be spaced and moved as needed during the swim.

Notes Regarding Boats

All boats shall be captained by a United States Coast Guard (USCG) qualified captain. All boats shall be equipped with operative GPS, radar and marine radio.

Other Craft Involved

There may be other craft involved in the swim, including San Francisco Police Department (SFPD) Marine Division, USCG and media boats.

The SFPD and USCG are very professional and are there to assist swimmers as needed. The media boats are there for the sole purpose of gathering news and pictures. They can become a problem, interfering with the swim by inadvertently leading front swimmers off course. The conduct of the media boats must be monitored and controlled

There is also a Ferry for transporting swimmers to the start near Alcatraz. The Race Director is on board the Ferry, and with the concurrence of the Swim Director decides on the time and place for the start. After the start of the swim the ferry departs.

Vessel Communications

There are three redundant levels of communication.

Marine Radio - All boats on the water are to be in communication via a predetermined marine radio channel which shall be monitored by all boats at all times.

Ham Radio Operator - The Command Boat, the Medical Boat, the Kayak Boat, the Lead Boat, both Flankers, the Ferry and at least one Sweeper shall have a ham radio operator on board. Hams will operate on a predetermined frequency, keeping in network contact with hams on the beach and the ferry in addition to the boats.

Cell Phone - Key personnel shall also have cell telephones, kept in the ON position, and be aware of each other's cell phone numbers.

The Command Boat will maintain contact with the USCG Vessel Traffic Control and with the SFPD vessels, including announcing the start, the progress and the finish of the swim.

Handling Swimmers in Trouble

Watercraft personnel shall constantly monitor the surrounding water for troubled swimmers and for raised kayak paddles. If a swimmer either needs or wants to be taken from the water, they are to be assisted on board the boat and made comfortable. If there are signs of a medical situation, the Medical Boat is to be summoned immediately, and, if necessary, the SFPD boat.

In the event that a swimmer is in a position that will prevent them from completing the swim (too far back, left or right) that swimmer must be *strongly advised and required* to enter the boat under penalty of disqualification for refusal to do so.

It has been the policy of race management to allow swimmers, who have been taken into a boat for any reason, the option of returning to the water to rejoin the swim in a position more advantageous to the swimmer. Swimmers are also permitted to remain on board the boat should they opt **not** to re-enter the water. The race number of swimmer[s] opting **not** to re-enter the water must be provided to the swim director.

MEDICAL PROTOCOL: ON THE WATER

There shall be a 'Medical Boat' on the water manned by a medical professional, the Medical Coordinator, and a CPR trained California Certified Lifeguard, an experienced pilot, a ham operator and an assistant. All medical situations on the water are to be referred by all boats to the Medical Coordinator. In addition, CPR trained California Certified Lifeguards are on several motorized vessels.

On the Beach

There shall be a properly staffed ambulance on alert near the swim finish, ready to accept patients from the Medical Coordinator as needed during and after the race. A medical professional shall be at the swim finish at all times, hired by Race Director.

Relationship with SFPD Personnel

We are fortunate to have SFPD and sometimes USCG craft attending the swim. We are to accept their help as necessary and as offered and defer to them when appropriate.

Relationship with Beach Medical Personnel

The medical personnel on the beach shall be kept advised of any medical situations on the water which may require the use of shoreside medical personnel or ambulance. Communcation will be via ham radio.

Communications

There shall be ham radio operators on the Medical Boat and on the beach at the swim finish in contact with medical personnel in both locations, transferring information as needed. Ham radio operators shall also immediately advise the Swim Director and Race Director of medical situations.

Location of Medical Boat

For most of the swim the Medical Boat will stay to the rear of the swim, with the slower swimmers and the sweepers. As the swim progresses, it will relocate as needed.

GARY'S ACKNOWLEDGMENTS

It has taken me nearly 60 years to gain the experience to write this book. Along the way, many people have supported me, extended a mentoring hand and helped me achieve my goals - they deserve more than the brief acknowledgment afforded them here.

Thanks to my father, Edgar, who taught me how to swim before I learned to walk; and to Janice, my mother, who instilled in me a sense and belief that I can accomplish anything as long as I put my mind to it (and to whomever gave me the genes that encourage my tendency towards excess – an extra thanks!).

Ron Buss, my first swim coach, I still can't believe you came by to pick me up at 5:00 a.m. that entire summer for those early morning swim work-outs (I also can't believe I actually got up at 5:00 a.m. during my summer vacation to work-out). Gene Del Gaudio, thanks for four years of high school coaching and for helping me perfect my swimming technique, lap after lap after lap.

Dave Horning of Envirosports, thanks for taking an enthusiastic neophyte Alcatraz swimmer under your wings and teaching me to never stop looking at the myriad possibilities out there.

Joe Oakes, thanks for adopting me as a surrogate son (or is that younger brother), for teaching me the ropes of the business (long live the *Alcatraz Challenge Aquathlon & Swim*), for drafting me to come along on so many exotic adventures and for being my friend.

"Stevie Ray" Hurwitz and Pedro Ordenes (a.k.a as "Tuna"), thanks (I think) for always trying to stay one Alcatraz swim ahead of me and for "forcing" me into all those afternoon "bump 'n run" Alcatraz swims on our run up to 500 crossings. It's still a toss-up who will get to 1,000 first!

To the members of the *Alcatraz Swimming Society* (ASS): Dianna Shuster, Kristine "Bucko" Buckley, Allen Luong, Joe Butler, Paul Saab and Stevie Ray for our weekly Wednesday morning Alcatraz swims (it beats sitting around playing canasta). And to Lee Block for keeping ASS grounded by reminding us our Alcatraz swims don't mean squat and that we're nothing more than "Alcatrassholes."

Bob Roper, Jon Meyer, Darryl Hickey, Rick Weber and all the other pilots who take care of us when the water's calm and safe and who guard over us when the water, weather and vessel traffic conditions would keep saner swimmers landbound.

Brent Allen, thanks for taking a chance on me as an open-water coach and instructor, for persistently staying on my case until I wrote my first Alcatraz booklet and produced my DVD "Lane Lines to Shore Lines" and for convincing me I could turn my passion for open water swimming into a career as an "aquapreneur."

And most importantly, an infinite amount of thanks, undying gratitude and forever and for always love to my wife Peg who over the years not only has allowed me to pull her out of bed at 3:30 a.m. but has let me drag her all over the world so I can do yet another crazy swim with her standing by to identify my remains should anything go amiss. Thanks for your incredible support, behind the scenes grunt work and insistence on perfection that makes me look so much, much better than I really am.

JOE'S ACKNOWLEDGEMENTS

Thirty years ago Frank Drum, President of the Dolphin Club, supported me in my efforts to bring the infant sport of triathlon to San Francisco. I will always be indebted to him and to others at the Dolphin Club who helped to get my Alcatraz project off the ground. That beginning enabled Peter Butler, Sally Bailey and me to build what would become a San Francisco institution. With their hard work and integrity the Alcatraz project came to fruition, overcoming some big hurdles. We had to deal with more than our share of sleaze-bags, phonies and idiots.

Taking responsibility for the safety of thousands of swimmers in dangerous water requires the teamwork of dedicated and hard-working people. Among them are the standout performances of Captain Andy Guiliano, coordinator of the motorized fleet; Bob Stender and Marc Paulsen, who have built a team of kayak escorts unequaled anywhere; Barry Bettman, a genius when it comes to organizing radio communications; Cissy Chase, our on-water medical coordinator; Sue Free; George Rehmet; Danny Needham; Derek Elliot; and Faride Khalaf.

Huge thanks go to all of the swimmers from the South End Club who so often immersed themselves, almost naked, in the frigid waters of SF Bay to do our test swims. *Brrrrr!* The driving inspiration behind them has long been Bay swimming legend Bobby Roper.

When you are out on the water with responsibility for hundreds of swimmers it is comforting to know that the professionals are nearby in case the inevitable unexpected happens. I refer to the Coast Guard and the SFPD Marine Unit under the command of the knowledgeable and helpful Sgt. Danny Lopez.

Over the years I have been exposed to some remarkable coaches. I will single out Laurie 'Killifish' Kilbourne for her patience and understanding, and Joel Wilson for his depth of knowledge, his experience, and his ability to pass it on.

I want to thank my mother for allowing me to do things that she knew I shouldn't do, and Sylvia for biting her tongue so many times when I did things that frightened her. Thank you to Dan'l, Chris and Victoria for being Dan'l, Chris and Victoria.

John Morris-Reihl gets special kudos for his professional work in taking our raw manuscript and turning it into a book. Sylvia, my wife and inspiration, did a great job of editing it with a fine toothed comb.

Most of all, thanks go to my partner, Gary Emich, for his friendship, his patience and his cooperation.

PHOTO CREDITS

A special thanks to the following for allowing Joe and Gary to use their photographs (all other photos courtesy of Gary):

James Gaffney – www.KarenGaffneyFoundation.com – page 7

William Chinn – page 60

Peg Gerard – pages 38, 55, 85, 90, 96 (top) & 98

APPENDIX

Listed below are a few items that you might find interesting.

EVENTS: There are too many to include all of them, and they change from time to time. A few of our favorite open-water events are:

The Alcatraz Challenge Swim and Aquathlon. You swim from Alcatraz to Crissy Field then run across the Golden Gate Bridge and back. It is one of the most beautiful events in the Bay Area, and was rated as one of the top ten swims in the world a couple of years ago.

The Alcatraz Challenge Swim. This is a relatively new event that has grown out of the Alcatraz Challenge Swim and Aquathlon. It is a swim only event. You will find both of these events at www.tricalifornia.com.

The San Francisco Triathlon at Alcatraz. This event is also put on by Tri California. The swim from Alcatraz to the Marina Green is followed by a difficult bike ride and a picturesque run. Not for weenies.

The Alcatraz Invitational Swim. Produced by the South End Rowing Club, this is a classic event. After the swim you will be able to enjoy a (crowded) sauna and a great meal. www.south-end.org

The Roy Webster Cross-Channel Swim. This non-competitive crossing of the Columbia from Washington to Oregon has been going on longer (68 years) than most people have been alive. Put on by the Hood River, Oregon Chamber of Commerce. www.hoodriver.org

Roper Invitational Golden Gate Crossing. The currents, fog and uncertainty make this a tough one. Bob has been swimming and breaking records in the Bay since Moby Dick was a minnow (his 1968 17:21 minute record crossing of the GGB remains unbroken). www.roper(type-in-current year).eventbrite.com / e.g. if it's 2011, enter www.roper2011.eventbrite.com

The RCP Tiburon Mile. Bob Placak uses a large paycheck to lure some of the best open water swimmers in the world to this event. It is worth looking into. www.rcptiburonmile.com

Swim Across America San Francisco. This non-competitive swim goes from mid-span of the Golden Gate Bridge into the East Beach of Crissy Field. Funds raised from the non-profit event go to UCSF Children's Hospital and Children's Hospital Research Institute Oakland. www.swimacrossamerica.org

TransBay Relay Benefit Swim. Three-person relay teams and / or soloists swim 9 miles from Needles Rock (by the north tower of the Golden Gate Bridge) to the Emeryville Marina just north of Oakland. Funds raised from the non-profit event support Baykeeper, the environmental watchdog of San Francisco Bay. Without Baykeeper, we wouldn't be able to swim in a non-polluted Bay. www.baykeeper.org

OPEN WATER VENUES IN AND AROUND SAN FRANCISCO.

Most of the City's waterfront is built up, with almost no access for swimming, but there are a few golden places still open to you in and around the City.

Aquatic Park. Once around the Cove is just short of a mile but be careful because the Cove is not immune to currents and wind chop. Before you go in, look at what the anchored boats in the Cove are doing: which way are they facing? Take a look at the flags and see how the wind is blowing. A shorter swim in the Cove, about a half mile, is back and forth along the full length of the marker buoys parallel to the beach. Aquatic Park is located on the north end of Van Ness Avenue. Parking can be difficult. Showers are located at the east end of the Cove.

Candlestick Point State Recreation Area by the San Francisco 49-er's football stadium offers protected swimming with little to no current.

China Camp - McNear's Beach County Park in San Rafael offers nice swimming with the water temperature usually a few degrees warmer than Aquatic Park. Watch out for rocks getting in and out of the water and be aware there can be mild to moderate currents.

Clipper Cove located at Treasure Island offers protected swimming from the sandy beach (south western corner of the Cove) – keep an eye out for boat traffic in and out of the marina.

Clothing optional beaches: there are several of them, the most popular east of the "sand ladder" at Baker Beach (west of the Golden Gate Bridge). If your tastes go in that direction who are we to object?

Coyote Point Recreation Area in San Mateo offers relatively safe open water swimming with wind generating choppy conditions most afternoons (a good place to practice for Alcatraz). Located off Highway 101 close to SFO.

Crissy Field is two miles west of Aquatic Park and has a beautiful mile-long beach and toilet facilities. Joe doesn't like to swim there because the currents can really rip parallel to the beach, and because fast-moving wind-surfers make swimming dicey. It is worthwhile to take a look it because that is where some of the Alcatraz swims finish up. (It is best at slack and at neap tides.)

Ocean Beach is *NOT* recommended. Dangerous rip-currents drown unwary bathers every year.

Paradise Beach County Park in Tiburon is a very nice setting with water temperatures usually a few degrees warmer than Aquatic Park. Watch out for rocks getting in and out of the water and be aware that there are mild to moderate currents.

Pillar Point Harbor is about 3 miles north of Half Moon Bay and offers safe swimming. Jump in behind Sam's Chowder House but stay very clear of the boat ramp area.

USEFUL CONTACT INFORMATION

The South End Rowing Club (founded in 1873) is located at 500 Jefferson, just to the west of Fisherman's Wharf. Joe and Gary are both members. The Club has handball courts, a variety of boats, a gym, a running program and the best group of swimmers in America. It is a great place to take a swim from a private beach and use the showers and sauna to warm up afterwards. If you develop a liking for it, membership will cost you less than a health club and you get a beach to boot. Over the years we have developed many friendships there. $6.50 day-use fee – bring your own towel. www.south-end.org

The Dolphin Club, another club filled with tradition, adjacent to the South End Club. There are similarities and differences, but we are definitely prejudiced in favor of the SERC. www.dolphinclub.org

The Olympic Club, still another great SF club, hosts the annual Trans Tahoe Swim Relay - best if you are a golfer but they have a wide array of offerings: Pricey. www.olyclub.org

The Golden Gate Triathlon Club helps members achieve their athletic goals in a stimulating, supportive and sociable environment. www.ggtc.org

Water World Swims offers open water swimming events in San Francisco Bay as well as weekly group swims. www.waterworldswims.com

Swim Art offers year-round open water swimming programs in the San Francisco Bay and beyond. The offer weekly group swims, instructional clinics, and special Expedition swims in different locations. Good quality instruction in the weekly group swims.

www.swim-art.com

Swim Trek – the ultimate vacation for open water swimmers. Based in the UK, Swim Trek offers week-long swimming vacations throughout Europe, in the British Virgin Islands and in Baja Mexico. www.swimtrek.com

Pacific Masters Swimming hosts a very popular Northern California open water swim event circuit each year. http://www.open-waterpacific.org

US Open Water Swimming provides a comprehensive calendar of open water swim events as well as safe places to swim across the U.S. www.openwaterswimming.org

The Water is Open provides the latest on open water swimming news and events throughout the world www.thewaterisopen.org

Ocean Swims provides a complete list of open water events, articles and happenings "down-under." If you're heading to Australia this is the site to check out. www.oceanswims.com

The San Francisco Police Bureau, Marine Unit, is currently under the direction of Sgt. Danny Lopez. They are great people to have on your side out on the water.

The United States Coast Guard is the organization that issues permits for events in the Bay. If you are planning to do a swim outside Aquatic Cove, you will need a permit. They are also on call to handle marine emergencies.

BACKGROUND READING, VIEWING:

If you want to make the transition from pool swimmer to open water swimming, there is no better way to approach the subject than the DVD *Lane Lines to Shore Lines: Your Complete Guide to Open Water Swimming,* available at www.lanelinestoshorelines.com.

A good adventure read is ***With a Single Step*** - the true story of Joe's non-motorized circumnavigation of the earth. He swam, ran, walked, bicycled, sailed, climbed, kayaked all the way around the world. It is available at www.josephoakes.com and www.lanelines-toshorelines.com.

Escape from Alcatraz – the book by J. Campbell Bruce that was made into the popular movie starring Clint Eastwood is available at numerous online sites.

Wet Poets' Society – an anthology of swimmers' poetry and art (contributors include such famous swimming legends as Alison Streeter and Lynne Cox) is available at www.wetpoetssociety.com

Wind, Waves and Sunburn – this classic history of marathon swimming by Conrad Wennerberg is available at numerous online sites.

History of Open-water Marathon Swimming – a comprehensive history of open water swimming during the past 200 years - www.captainsengsvc.com.

GLOSSARY

The terms listed below are related to the tides, currents and open water swimming in general. It is by no means a complete glossary.

Tides are the vertical (up and down) movements of the sea. They are caused by the gravitational pull of the moon and, to a lesser extent, the sun. In San Francisco Bay there are typically two high tides and two low tides each day. The greatest tidal action occurs at the new moon and the full moon because of the co-linearity of the earth, moon and sun. The smallest tidal action occurs at the neap tides, halfway between the new moon and the full moon. A large tidal swing between high and low in the Bay may be as much as eight feet.

Current is the horizontal movement of the surface water. In San Francisco Bay it is the result of both the action of the tides and the outflow of the Sacramento and San Joaquin river systems. It follows that the largest currents occur when there is greatest tidal movement, the full and new moons. A strong ebbing current may reach over seven nautical miles per hour (that's nearly eight miles an hour for you land-lubbers). That is a lot faster than the strongest swimmer can match.

Ebb currents refer to the westward movement of the water in the Bay, flowing out the Golden Gate into the Pacific. During the ebb the level of the Bay decreases. Remember the ebb empties the Bay.

Flood currents move eastward from the Pacific through the Golden Gate. The result of the flood is to increase the height of the water level in the Bay. Remember the flood fills the Bay.

Slack current, erroneously called 'slack tide', is that brief time when the Bay currents reverse from an ebbing current to a flooding current or vice versa.

Note that because of the complexity of the Bay, tides and currents occur at different times and in different locations. For example, much of what happens at the Golden Gate might have happened a half hour earlier just south of Alcatraz.

Tide Tables are handy tools for the determination of tides and currents in the Bay. The reference location is the Golden Gate, and there are correction factors for many locations in the Bay and the Sacramento Delta. The tides and currents are listed by date, time and location. They are available from commercial sources and from the original source, the Federal Government. There are two common methods of presenting tidal information. One is strictly tabular, the other in the form of daily sinusoidal graphs. Both have their advantages. The data represented in these tables are the result of years of observations at data recording stations located throughout the Bay. (Tide tables are also available for many locations in US waters, and internationally.)

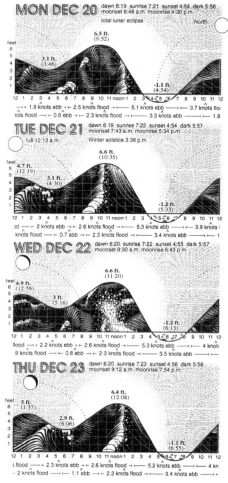

Sinusoidal Tide Table

DECEMBER
TIDES AT GOLDEN GATE, CALIFORNIA – 2010
Heights in feet · Pacific Standard Time

Moon	Day		Time	Ht.	Time	Ht.	Time	Ht.	Time	Ht.
			LOW		HIGH		LOW		HIGH	
	1	Wed	0035	1.5	0726	6.3	1404	0.1	2040	4.3
	2	Thr	0130	1.9	0808	6.6	1454	-0.6	2148	4.5
	3	Fri	0223	2.3	0850	6.8	1541	-1.0	2248	4.7
	4	Sat	0314	2.6	0933	6.8	1626	-1.3	2341	4.9
●S	5	Sun	0404	2.8	1015	6.8	1709	-1.4		
			HIGH		LOW		HIGH		LOW	
	6	Mon	0031	4.9	0452	2.9	1057	6.6	1752	-1.3
	7	Tue	0117	4.9	0541	3.0	1140	6.3	1833	-1.1
	8	Wed	0202	4.9	0632	3.1	1223	6.0	1915	-0.7
	9	Thr	0246	4.9	0726	3.1	1307	5.6	1957	-0.3
	10	Fri	0328	4.9	0826	3.0	1355	5.1	2040	0.1
	11	Sat	0409	4.9	0932	2.9	1448	4.6	2123	0.6
EA○	12	Sun	0447	5.0	1043	2.6	1552	4.1	2209	1.1
	13	Mon	0524	5.1	1150	2.2	1710	3.7	2258	1.6
	14	Tue	0600	5.3	1249	1.7	1840	3.6	2348	2.0
	15	Wed	0636	5.5	1339	1.1	2006	3.6		
			LOW		HIGH		LOW		HIGH	
	16	Thr	0040	2.4	0713	5.7	1422	0.6	2115	3.9
	17	Fri	0130	2.7	0751	5.9	1502	0.1	2211	4.1
	18	Sat	0217	2.9	0830	6.1	1539	-0.4	2257	4.4
N	19	Sun	0302	3.0	0911	6.4	1616	-0.8	2339	4.6
○P	20	Mon	0346	3.1	0952	6.5	1654	-1.1		
			HIGH		LOW		HIGH		LOW	
	21	Tue	0019	4.7	0430	3.1	1035	6.6	1733	-1.2
	22	Wed	0058	4.9	0516	3.0	1120	6.6	1813	-1.2
	23	Thr	0137	5.0	0606	2.9	1208	6.4	1855	-1.1
	24	Fri	0217	5.2	0701	2.7	1259	6.1	1939	-0.8
	25	Sat	0258	5.4	0804	2.5	1355	5.5	2024	-0.3
E	26	Sun	0341	5.6	0914	2.2	1501	4.9	2112	0.4
○	27	Mon	0425	5.8	1029	1.7	1619	4.3	2204	1.0
	28	Tue	0511	6.1	1144	1.1	1753	4.0	2301	1.7
	29	Wed	0559	6.3	1252	0.4	1930	3.9		
			LOW		HIGH		LOW		HIGH	
	30	Thr	0004	2.2	0649	6.5	1353	-0.2	2052	4.2
	31	Fri	0107	2.6	0740	6.6	1446	-0.6	2157	4.5

December 21 = Solstice

LUNAR DATA
● = NEW MOON   ◑ = LAST QUARTER   N = FARTHEST NORTH OF EQUATOR
◐ = FIRST QUARTER   A = IN APOGEE   E = ON EQUATOR
○ = FULL MOON   P = IN PERIGEE   S = FARTHEST SOUTH OF EQUATOR

34

DECEMBER
CURRENTS AT GOLDEN GATE ENTRANCE 2010
SOUTH OF PT. DIABLO

Currents in Knots · Pacific Standard Time

Day	Slack	MAX Current Time H.M.	Vel Knots	Slack	MAX Current Time H.M.	Vel Knots	Slack	MAX Current Time H.M.	Vel Knots	Slack	MAX Current Time H.M.	Vel Knots	Slack
1 Wed	0259	0600	3.2F	0902	1209	4.4E	1608	1906	3.4F	2213			
2 Thr		0036	2.5E	0353	0651	3.1F	0946	1301	4.9E	1701	2005	3.8F	2317
3 Fri		0135	2.4E	0445	0740	3.1F	1031	1351	5.3E	1752	2059	4.1F	
4 Sat	0015	0230	2.3E	0536	0828	3.0F	1117	1440	5.4E	1841	2149	4.2F	
5 Sun	0109	0321	2.2E	0625	0916	2.9F	1202	1526	5.4E	1928	2237	4.2F	
6 Mon	0159	0408	2.1E	0714	1002	2.7F	1248	1612	5.3E	2015	2323	4.0F	
7 Tue	0246	0454	2.0E	0802	1048	2.6F	1333	1657	5.0E	2101			
8 Wed		0008	3.8F	0332	0539	2.0E	0852	1136	2.3F	1419	1742	4.7E	2146
9 Thr		0052	3.6F	0417	0625	2.0E	0946	1225	2.1F	1507	1827	4.2E	2230
10 Fri		0136	3.3F	0501	0712	2.0E	1044	1317	1.8F	1559	1914	3.7E	2315
11 Sat		0220	3.0F	0544	0801	2.1E	1146	1414	1.7F	1657	2003	3.2E	
12 Sun	0000	0305	2.8F	0625	0852	2.3E	1250	1516	1.6F	1802	2054	2.8E	
13 Mon	0045	0349	2.6F	0706	0943	2.5E	1351	1623	1.7F	1912	2149	2.3E	
14 Tue	0132	0435	2.4F	0745	1034	2.9E	1448	1730	1.9F	2023	2245	2.0E	
15 Wed	0220	0520	2.3F	0824	1124	3.2E	1539	1831	2.2F	2129	2341	1.8E	
16 Thr	0307	0605	2.3F	0904	1212	3.7E	1626	1925	2.5F	2230			
17 Fri		0036	1.7E	0354	0649	2.3F	0943	1259	4.1E	1710	2012	2.9F	2325
18 Sat		0128	1.7E	0438	0733	2.3F	1023	1344	4.5E	1753	2055	3.2F	
19 Sun	0015	0216	1.8E	0521	0816	2.4F	1103	1429	4.8E	1834	2137	3.5F	
20 Mon	0102	0303	1.9E	0603	0900	2.5F	1144	1513	5.1E	1915	2218	3.7F	
21 Tue	0147	0349	2.0E	0646	0944	2.6F	1226	1558	5.3E	1957	2300	3.9F	
22 Wed	0231	0436	2.2E	0732	1030	2.6F	1312	1644	5.3E	2039	2342	4.0F	
23 Thr	0314	0523	2.3E	0824	1119	2.6F	1401	1731	5.2E	2122			
24 Fri		0026	4.0F	0357	0612	2.6E	0921	1212	2.6F	1455	1820	4.9E	2207
25 Sat		0111	3.9F	0440	0703	2.8E	1025	1310	2.5F	1556	1912	4.3E	2253
26 Sun		0159	3.7F	0523	0756	3.1E	1133	1414	2.4F	1706	2007	3.7E	2343
27 Mon		0248	3.4F	0606	0852	3.5E	1244	1524	2.5F	1824	2106	3.1E	
28 Tue	0035	0341	3.2F	0652	0949	3.8E	1352	1639	2.7F	1943	2209	2.5E	
29 Wed	0132	0436	2.9F	0740	1049	4.2E	1456	1754	3.0F	2100	2315	2.1E	
30 Thr	0232	0533	2.8F	0830	1147	4.5E	1556	1902	3.3F	2211			
31 Fri		0023	1.9E	0332	0629	2.7F	0921	1244	4.8E	1651	2001	3.7F	2313

35

Tabular Tide Table

San Francisco Bay is not a bay at all but the estuary at the conjunction of the Pacific Ocean with the effluent of the Sacramento and San Joaquin Rivers which drain almost 1,000 miles of the Sierra Nevada Mountains. (As an aside, the State of California receives more snow than any other state. It is that snowmelt that creates the two great rivers that form San Francisco Bay.)

The Golden Gate is the mile-wide opening that separates San Francisco Bay from the Pacific Ocean. Bounded north and south by high promontories, it is located at the northwestern corner of San Francisco.

Alcatraz Island is a small, rocky outcropping of desolate rock in San Francisco Bay. It is located about two kilometers north of the South End Rowing Club. Ferries take tourists to Alcatraz several times a day. Alcatraz is the reason we wrote this book.

CPSIA information can be obtained
at www.ICGtesting.com
Printed in the USA
BVHW03s1212190518
516743BV00021B/166/P